Letters from the Pacific
49 Days on a Cargo Ship

Sandra Shaw Homer

To all Seafarers –
whether on the wide oceans
or in their hearts.

A man, a plan, a canal, Panama.

Anonymous palindrome

Table of Contents

Prologue
Do I really have to do this?

It's never been about the destinations, this freighter voyage, exotic though they may be. It's been something less tangible than being able to say I sat on a beach on the International Date Line or saw a wombat in Australia.

No, for me it's about the ocean – those long stretches across the wide Pacific, with no land in sight, endless water in all directions, sky and sea one liquid element, stormy or calm – that I want to see, perched in the bow as we plow into . . . nothingness. The churn of the engines at the stern, the steady slap of the waves against the hull, the open-ended silence of the sea.

It's also been about escape: finding myself in a new medium where I could breathe a different air, feel a new breeze on my cheek, think new thoughts. There will be new people, probably new nationalities and new languages. This also makes me nervous; what if nobody speaks English or Spanish? Just in case, I've been boning up on my 50-year-old high school French, but it's harder at this age.

I think of my grandmother, Leora, a divorced lady of a certain age, missing her "man from Thomas Cooke" at the train station, making her own way to the hotel without benefit of language, finding her room not ready yet, and stepping into the Ladies' and reapplying her lipstick, her "red badge of courage." I think of her in every country she traveled, charming everyone she met.

I'm thinking of my mother, too, another traveler. The first time she was invited to accompany her mother-in-law, she had to handle the luggage . . . and Leora had packed 17 dresses! This motivated my mother to perfect a leaner style: "Never pack more than you can carry yourself." She prepared for each voyage, right down to the block-by-block walking tours and the old language LPs. It was important to her to be able to walk a city street and look like she knew where she was going. She was innately shy. As am I.

That kind of *grand tour* travel is too uncomfortable for me now, so a sea voyage seems like the perfect way to go somewhere without all the trouble of getting there. The ship moves; I stay put. The big cruise ships don't appeal. I've seen them at the dock in Costa Rican ports; they look so top-heavy, they can't possibly be seaworthy! Once, waiting for a friend to disembark from one of these monsters, I begged the deck officer to let me on board so I could use a ladies' room (it was a long walk back to land-based services). He relaxed the rules and ushered me into a small, deeply carpeted lobby with elevators on either side, just like any hotel anywhere on the planet. Nothing ship-like about it.

Nor am I interested in gambling, musical comedy or 24-hour-a-day food. Traveling is more than just plunking yourself down somewhere to eat and be entertained. It's the feeling of motion, of going-to, of discovering that thing inside you that responds to things new. It's *opening the door* – to the inside, as well as out.

Ah, why didn't I think to mention my father? How I prefer to think of my female relatives first! But I certainly carry his ocean genes. He was no great traveler, but the sea was his element, and he was truly happiest at the tiller or wheel, it didn't matter on what body of water. It was sitting cross-legged in the bow of my father's only yawl (an Alden boat, he would tell you) that I first felt the joy of being afloat in the vast, undefined watery spaces.

Not long ago, a friend told me about a solitary retreat she had taken on a remote Pacific beach. I asked her for any thoughts that might help guide me on my upcoming voyage. She wrote:

"You are indeed looking at a long time at sea, and the first and middle weeks will probably be hard. Once you get quiet, however, it may be amazing. Whatever it is – hard or amazing – just keep looking inward for what the moment has to teach you."

How wonderful to have such wise friends! I sensed there was a goal knocking around in my head somewhere, but I never could have put it so beautifully. So, this voyage on the cargo ship *Louise** that I board at the northern end of the Panama Canal, with stops in Papeete (Tahiti), Lautoka (Fiji), Noumea (New Caledonia, excuse me, *Nouvelle Caledonie*), Sydney, Melbourne (Australia), Napier and Tauranga (New Zealand), then returning over two weeks' worth of unopposed, open ocean to Panama – a trip of 49 days in all – will be a voyage of exploration. Although I know

2

which ports – the destinations – I will see, I have no idea where this journey will lead, no clear sense of what I'm looking for. All I know is that I *will* be looking. That's a start.

*Although I have changed the names for courtesy's sake, everything that follows is true.

Passage One
Costa Rica to Tahiti via Panama
The Canal and Beyond

June 22, The Journey Begins: Neither my husband nor I had been farther south than Quepos, so it was all new country, and the Costa Rican coast there gets wilder and freer of development. Inland we passed endless miles of oil palm plantations, broken occasionally by clearings where the old wooden stilt houses were built around soccer fields, worker housing back in the days when the land was still dedicated to bananas. There is a certain grace to these old structures compared to the stuffy cement-block boxes the companies build for them now, a better understanding then of the climatic conditions – heavy rains, flooding, the need to be up in the air to catch a breeze.

The border was not as bad as the Nicaraguan border, which took us four hours years ago during Christmas week, and I'm glad we had the advice of friends to immediately accept the help of an unofficial guide. It would have taken hours longer without Ruben, a Panamanian who's been steering people through the stages of the frontier crossing for seventeen years. He was amiable and efficient, but there were a couple of stops – out of nine separate offices we had to visit! – where the officials were just mean.

Roger had remarked during the drive south how few big trucks we encountered. We found them all at the border, lined up on either side for several kilometers, some of their drivers dangling in hammocks slung under their trailers, others doing laundry in buckets or smoking and chatting with each other. They were striking on both sides of the border because of a new $25 fumigation fee. Just as we arrived, the strike was resolved and they started coming through, putting tremendous pressure on the Immigration and Customs officials to process them quickly. So it's not surprising some of them were feeling impatient by the middle of the afternoon.

Finally fumigated ourselves (for one dollar), we broke out for the city of David, which is when I realized I had forgotten to ask our friends how to find our hotel –somehow I'd managed to leave home without even a phone number! It had taken us six hours to reach the border, another hour to cross and a further hour to find the hotel, which fortunately was right on the central square. The room was meager, the food mediocre, and the management less than welcoming, but everything was clean and the staff in the dining room amiable. This is where we tried to sleep through our first noisy air conditioner. It's sweaty-hot in David, even on a cloudy morning, which it was the next day when we went in search of an ATM machine. We strolled briefly around the beautifully landscaped central park, the only break in a wilderness of ugly commercial clutter and fuel exhaust, and then we climbed into the car for the next leg.

I am grateful to Roger for taking on this drive. There were no flights from San José to Colón, and those to Panama City were ridiculously expensive. Even if I had flown, I would have had the difficulties of getting myself and some heavy luggage to the other side of the country (train? bus? taxi?) where the Manzanillo International Terminal is. A good part of the reason for choosing to sail over any other way of getting to exotic places was my physical discomfort on planes and in airports, but even in a car, with the ability to stop and move around at will, the arthritis pained me for all but the first few hours of the trip.

Roger, I find, likes to travel to new places only if he's driving. He speeds on down the road, looking from side to side, cheery and voluble as I rarely see him. On the Coastal Starlight between Los Angeles and Seattle – a 36-hour train trip past some of the most beautiful scenery in the States – he quickly became bored and buried himself in a book. The only couple of times we've traveled together he hasn't been the pleasantest of companions, so I long ago stopped suggesting we go anywhere. Early in my search for a ship, I had come across a week's cruise in the Caribbean on the largest sailing ship in the world – he likes boats. But when I asked him if he'd like to go, he actually said, "It would depend on what's going on around here." Still, I felt bound to ask him if he wanted to go on this Pacific voyage, and he said he would be bored to death for 49 days at sea. I was secretly relieved.

I suspect he knew it was important for me to go alone.

On the Road: Back on the Pan-American – now just a two-lane road, meandering through hilly country with long views of the blue mountains to the north – we saw few visible signs of human activity and even fewer services along the way. We passed some thatched sheds where native women were selling colorful dresses, and we saw one ox-cart laboring along the shoulder, but at no point were we out of sight of a mobile phone tower, which we observed with the all the irony that only the technologically deprived can feel. Then from Santiago east, things got busier, the road two lanes in both directions with hectare upon hectare of sugar cane fields whizzing by on either side of us.

I'm having more frequent I-can't-believe-I'm-really-doing-this moments.

From David to our hotel at the very tip of old Colón, with only a brief lunch-stop, took a total of seven hours. Tropical downpours threatened as we came down into the city under a grim sky. There's no traffic control in Colón and, as in many ex-colonial cities, street planning broke down as it spilled out of its original grid layout. Not one stop sign, not one traffic light, a pure Latino free-for-all. The central avenue had once been elegant – long blocks of two and three-story buildings with balconies overhanging the street, a broad center island filled with trees and park benches. But the whole is suffering a kind of jungle rot – crumbling balustrades, peeling paint, clothes hanging limply on lines stretched any-which-way across the facades, television antennas tilting dizzily out over the street. Grizzled old men, street-dwellers, were washing their clothes at hydrants in the park.

The Hotel New Washington is a wonderful old architectural wreck, seedy, dirty in the corners and reminiscent of a Graham Greene novel, but still offering a front-row view of 30 or so freighters awaiting cargos in Limón Bay. More mediocre food and indifferent management; Panamanians don't seem to be as friendly as Costa Ricans. There was a wireless Internet connection that was available only in the hall, but there were tables and chairs so one could be comfortable.

Getting Oriented: We came to Panama without a roadmap or even enough U.S. dollars (which are on a par with the Panamanian dollar), but from checking on line it seemed there were only two principal roads: the Pan-American Highway running more or less parallel with the south coast, a continuation of what is called the *Inter-Americana* in Costa Rica, so we figured we could find it, and the north-south *autopista,* a new super-highway east of the Canal, leading from Panama City north to Colón. How could we get lost? Our friends had counseled us that the Miraflores locks were worth a look, so we asked at our hotel breakfast how to find them, little knowing they were all the way on the other side of the country. One waiter wasn't sure. Another waiter gave us somewhat clearer directions to what turned out to be the Gatún locks, which were worth a visit too, especially since there were two ships passing through at the same moment. There was also a gift shop where a knowledgeable young lady sold us a roadmap and set us straight, and off we went back across the country, an hour and fifteen minutes away. Twice we went over the incredibly beautiful new *Puente Centenario,* Centennial Bridge, before we found friendly security officials and traffic cops who were happy to guide us to Mireflores, because there were no signs until you were right on top of it.

The visitor center at Miraflores is a five-story building right on the Canal, and we started with an early lunch on the shaded deck on the third floor. No ships, but lots of interesting things to look at, including a small control building between the east and west passages with the date of 1913. The Canal was inaugurated two years later. We heard over the p.a. system that traffic moved through in only one direction at a time, which makes sense, as it's obviously a tricky operation and traffic control in both directions would be a lot trickier. (The best reading on the history and engineering of the Canal is *The Path between the Seas* by David McCullough, which hugely enhanced our appreciation for the real thing.) Eventually, the ships started to stack up in the small lake between Pedro Miguel and Miraflores locks, and an oil tanker and a grain ship were first to come through. The lowering of the water level seems to take less time than the rising, at least it seems to happen quite fast. (That was my impression later on shipboard, too.)

Our overwhelming impression of the Canal Zone was of the battle between human development and a formidable environment – how did they ever dig through all these mountains and jungles? And they're still digging – widening and dredging the channels, building new locks each the size of four football fields, laying new super highways – digging, digging, digging all over the Zone. There are whole mountainsides of bare dirt, terraced and drained to try to control erosion. We had passed through some stretches of national park on our drive, and we recognized what we were looking at, because there are places at home like these – dense, unforgiving tropical jungles – and I kept thinking that, once abandoned, all these great human works would quickly disintegrate and disappear in an overwhelming tide of green.

Boarding: I went down to the hotel pool this morning, while Roger searched out the route to the port – he didn't want any surprises late in the day when we would have to get there through who-knew-what traffic, and I didn't want to spend any more time in the car. The pool attendant was vacuuming, but I asked if I could swim anyway, since I had observed the day before that he threw the chemicals in right after the cleaning, and I didn't feel like a chlorine bath. We agreed I could swim where he had already vacuumed, as long as I didn't roil up the water too much.

It was delicious, the water perfect, a soothing balm for all my aches. On one of my luxurious lolling laps over to the far corner from the ladder, I suddenly noticed the vacuum pump perched on the edge of the coping, a long electric extension cable stretching off to somewhere, bare wires barely a foot above the water. It was a real Latin-American moment; apparently Ralph Nader hasn't discovered Panama yet either. I'm sure the attendant had no idea of the danger . . . or maybe he did. Whatever, after a shudder, I smiled at myself and kept swimming. It just felt too good.

Late in the afternoon, with almost no traffic at all, we met the port agent on time, after a series of friendly guards had directed us to the correct unmarked building. All it took was a quick pass of my passport through the computer and a stamp, and the agent handed my luggage through the security gate and I was in a hot jitney weaving its way through towering stacks of containers. There was no long-distance view of the *Louise* at the dock; the containers crowded in too close. All I saw was a pair of Filipino crew members with big grins on their faces clattering down the accommodation ladder to fetch my heavy cases. I was apparently expected to follow them up the shaky structure, and so I grasped the thick cable that served as a handrail, discovered it was coated with black grease, and wondered why I had ever had the notion to wear white slacks. Up on the main deck I had to sign in, and the one with the skinny black mustache, blue jumpsuit and hard-hat spoke enough Spanish to get me officially on board. The young Steward who took over from there didn't, but he led me onto an elevator and up to E Deck, where he deposited me in the Owner's Cabin and left me to unpack. Plenty of room to stow everything, including a hanging locker that locked, a desk with a comfortable chair, two beds, a sofa, my own bath and space to lay out my yoga mat on the floor. Décor: Freighter Functional? It's a working boat, after all. And now, after all the months of planning and anticipation and anxiety about this voyage, I am exhausted but finally aboard.

Our good-byes came too quickly. I had hoped Roger could accompany me to the ship and see me off, but outside the Immigration office we learned that he would not be able to follow me through security, and I had to go on alone. I had wanted to tell him something for several days, but it's almost impossible to find the right moment between us for these kinds of intimacies. I had wanted to tell him that I now understand that whenever I make him feel inadequate, it's only because I am feeling inadequate myself. But there we were standing awkwardly with the port agent and suddenly realizing we had no more time; we hugged goodbye, and the words went unsaid. I regret this.

At six, the designated dinner hour, I found my way by the interior stairs down to B Deck and the Officers' Mess, where I met one of the only two other passengers, a petite Swiss woman with short gray hair and expressive blue-gray eyes named Cristi, whose English, thank God, is wonderful, since I haven't dusted off any high school German since 1979. Our other passenger, Lila, was still ashore, and only one crew member – the tall, head-shaven electrician – came in briefly, saying in heavily accented English, "Good evening, good appetite" (the only words I heard out of him until the end of the voyage).

Day One, The Panama Canal: I find myself feeling simple joy just to be under way. Sitting in a folding chair up on F Deck, sliding past the jungly shores of Gatún Lake, watching bow line up with the shore-markers, carefully noting the buoys guarding the channel, feeling the swings into the wide turns, the sun bright on the olive-green water, just a few wisps of cloud in the sky and the clean scent of a breeze blowing . . . I'm happy!

When I boarded, it had been airless, Panamanian hot. I went to bed early, knowing that we would get under way sometime during the night, and at 1:30 I woke to the motion of the ship, threw on my jeans and went out on deck. There was little to see, of course – lights along the shore – but the motion felt good, the moving air felt good. I went back to bed and slept soundly until 4:30, when I knew we would be approaching the Canal. At 5:00, I was outside watching the dawn break over Port Cristobal, noting our progress into the approach channel.

Lila, who had boarded in New York, came out and introduced herself, and she went to wake Cristi so we could all watch our passage together. They came up with enough folding chairs for the three of us and we sat three abreast with our feet propped on the rail to enjoy the view. After we had passed the Gatún locks, Cristi said it was like taking a lake cruise, that it was difficult to imagine we were actually in a canal.

I couldn't watch all of the lock operations – the sun was just too bright – but I made sure to be on deck for the Miraflores run. It was fun hailing the tourists on the observation deck where Roger and I had been only two days before. I imagine some of them wondered what three middle-aged women were doing taking our ease on the deck of a container ship. But I was tired, and the arthritis everywhere began to hurt, especially in my knees from climbing up and down all these steep stairways – F Deck is just below the Bridge and one up from my cabin, and meals are served three decks down – so I went inside until we were exiting the Canal.

It doesn't take long aboard a cargo ship to realize that it's all about moving *things* – not people – from one part of the planet to another, and the scale is impressive. Last night I watched from the one of my two portholes (the one that isn't blocked by containers) as more of them were being loaded on board. In a port the size of Manzanillo, there are huge gantries on tracks that slide up and down the docks, lean out over the ships and then, with a crane that looks like a set of giant jaws, swoop containers up off the backs of trucks and up, up and over to the exact location on board where they belong. A crane operator way up under the gantry zips back and forth in his little glass cage operating the dozens of cables needed to control all this. I have to admire the skill and precision needed for such a task, just as I admire the drivers of the hefty little locomotives *(mulas)* that keep the ships in the Canal from banging into the sides or charging the gates, all by means of tow lines kept at just the right tension throughout the passage from one lock chamber to the next. I am still wide-eyed, but I sense that my view of freighter travel, gleaned from old Joseph Conrad novels, has been somewhat romanticized.

Almost 5:00 p.m., and we have left the glittering Oz-like towers of Panama City behind, along with a tropical downpour that is drenching the coast under a leaden curtain of cloud. We are finally at speed under a westering sun, generating a bow wave I can't see, only the roiling salt-milk vortexes it kicks up along the hull in the inky water. Cristi and I stand at the rail, watching the receding shore at day's end, both of us loving the free motion of the ship through the water, and we spot a couple of whales far off to starboard, breaking and blowing and slapping their tails, perhaps a mother and calf. What magic! Now we are chasing down the orange-hulled tanker that was just ahead of us in the last locks, passing a few humpy islands, leaving the sight of land behind for the next ten days. There's only a slight swell, but it will probably pick up the farther off-shore we go. I am at last heading into the unknown. Along with the joy, I feel a small trepidation at my heart.

At our first dinner at sea, Lila said that she and Cristi had both been awaiting the arrival of "the lady from Panama" with great curiosity. I guess to her that sounds about as exotic as her background does to me: she was born in Egypt but has lived in many other countries, and her English, too, is perfect. So all three of us are retired, within only a few years of each other in age, at least bilingual and well-traveled. How extraordinary to find three such women on a single freighter in the Pacific!

Day Two, at Sea: I woke to a sky and sea so equally gray you could barely see the difference. The decks are awash, and there's no incentive to go outside. This will be a good day to start to establish a routine – yesterday there was just too much to do! So after yoga, I went down to B Deck where the gym is mostly taken up with a Ping-Pong table and tried to figure out how to operate the bicycle and that multi-function machine that lets you pull up your legs, bring your arms together and lower a bar, all against weights. I was able to adjust the weights to something that was barely possible for me, but the tension on the bike was so great that I could force myself through only a few minutes at agonizingly slow speed. And I thought I was in pretty good shape for a woman of a certain age! If I make it through this, the cardiologist will finally be happy with me.

At lunch the Messman (who is also our Steward) told me that my visitor orientation session would begin at one o'clock, so I hurried up to my cabin to await Third Mate Denny. Except for the Captain, the Chief Engineer and the electrician, all from southeastern Europe, the crew is Filipino and, while all speak English to some degree, it's not easy to understand their accents over the noise of the engines or the air conditioning system, whichever predominates at the time. I certainly am not linguistically prepared for this trip! All are very courteous and, although the style on board is informal, they all call me ma'am. The funniest part of the orientation was the bright orange immersion suit, the donning of which Third Mate demonstrated to our mutual hilarity. This is a full-body rubber dry suit/flotation device that I could never get into unassisted but will keep me alive in a cold sea for who knows how long? The little flashing light attached to it is guaranteed to work for "eight hours or more." Reassuring.

Then I got the tour (except for the main deck and bow – it's blowing a Force 4 today, Third Mate told me), the most impressive part of which is the Bridge, two decks up. Here Second Mate Enrique, to whom I was introduced last night in his other persona as a karaoke singer, was the only one on watch. The Bridge is huge, extending the whole width of the ship, great downward-angled windows facing forward over the ranks of containers, massive banks of controls covered with unfathomable dials, lights and switches extending from starboard to port. Even with all this equipment, there's plenty of room on the Bridge for the whole crew of 19 and us three passengers to assemble in an emergency. I said to Third Mate that it was amazing to think our ancestors crossed these incredible ocean spaces 500 years ago with such crude navigation technology – they didn't even know where longitude was! And he said with a wide grin, "More technology, more paperwork." Second Mate told me we're still in Costa Rican territorial waters, and he showed me on the chart where we are, now just five degrees north of the Equator, but still on Costa Rica time. The typhoon, he said, is off the Mexican coast and heading northwest. (What typhoon? Nobody said anything about a typhoon.) We are safely heading *south*west, although the weather will continue gray and windy for the next day or so.

In the Captain's office, one deck down from the Bridge, is the ship-to-shore telephone (or do we now call it a sat-phone?) I can use ($21 for 40 minutes!), and the Captain graciously offered the use of the Master's exclusive email address for occasional communications with the outside world. I'll stick with Lila in port, as she too will be hunting down Internet cafés to stay in touch with family and friends. No one would want to impose on the Master of the ship, although he assured me that, now the Canal passage is behind us, everything can be much more relaxed. He told me his father had captained vessels on the banana run from Puerto Limón to the U.S. and that he had once shot a jaguar on a private Costa Rican farm – long ago when it was still legal, of course. Any talk of the Limón port brings up the subject of the worker syndicate there that habitually abused their collective bargaining agreement and shut the port down whenever they felt like it, causing multi-million-dollar losses to the shipping companies and the Costa Rican government; the ports were closed for all national holidays (including Mother's Day), the workers took exaggerated sick leave, and they struck for days on end whenever they wanted more concessions. Overcoming this situation was one of the signal successes of the Arias administration, later reversed, and I was surprised to learn from the Captain that French ports are just the same.

The Captain refers to us three passengers as "the ladies."

Third Mate then showed me the ship's office on A Deck, the large industrial laundry on B Deck, the various officers' Day Rooms, and a small room dedicated to the control of the trim of the ship. Trim, Denny explained, refers to the relative draft between bow and stern. If a ship is "by the stern" her aft end is lower in the water than her bow; if "on an even keel" both bow and stern are level; if she's "by the bow" she's in trouble. List is the radius of the roll, the degree to which she is leaning over on her side, which is what challenges your inner ear.

There is no level place to put anything down in the bathroom. The toilet sometimes takes two minutes (I'm counting while I hold down the handle) to flush. My shins have discovered the corner of every piece of furniture in the room. And the Captain likes a chilly ship: the temperature in my cabin has yet to exceed 73 F. I'm wearing long sleeves, and we're in the tropics!

As I was going in to dinner, I spotted Chief Engineer drinking a beer and having a cigarette in the Officers' Smoking and Recreation Lounge, just opposite the Mess. After I politely refused his offer of a drink, he hinted with no great subtlety at the importance of being social at sea: "Just as important as on land," he said. My big problem so far is everybody's smoking – well, just the passengers, Chief Engineer and electrician. But the four of them can fill up a lounge with smoke in just a few minutes, and, since I quit almost two years ago, I haven't been around this much smoke. My only worry is not the secondary smoke (I had plenty of primary smoke for 40 years), but the temptation to just pick a cigarette up off the bar and smoke it.

At dinner the captain told us the birds we are still seeing around the ship are, indeed, hitchhikers – they're sea hawks or sea eagles, and they roost somewhere on board at night. I would love to find their roost.

Day Three, at Sea: *I am remembering, as I look out at an almost full tropical moon and smell the sweet night as the sky begins to pale over the Pacific, that my father was in these waters at the end of the war. It was* *from a ship somewhere out here that he wrote that horrified letter to his Admiral after the bombs at Hiroshima and Nagasaki. In the letter, he sounds like an outraged, disillusioned youth – almost as if he hadn't yet seen Omaha Beach, with the bodies rolling in the surf and the shells screaming overhead. Maybe with Hiroshima, he finally had enough of killing and death. When I was growing up, he never talked about the war. Being here reminds me of this Pacific connection to him – pacific connection, after all the rage at his abuses – and it occurs to me that I would like to go through his papers once more. After he died, I could only skim them, didn't even want to touch them. Now, here, another notch in my ability to forgive him seems to have clicked into place. I go up to watch the sunrise from the observation deck. All alone out here, with nothing but the balm of a peaceful sea.*

E-mail to: *Roger, by way of the Captain's mail*
Subject: *Everything's fine*
Message: *Hello, love, I tried a number of times to call you on the sat-phone yesterday, but I kept receiving the recorded message that the number wasn't available. It occurs to me now that maybe our monopoly phone company isn't yet set up to handle modern satellite communications????? I was disappointed to learn that I'll only be able to communicate through the Captain's email address, so I don't want to impose on him too much. Another passenger, Lila, and I will be looking for Internet cafés wherever we can, so I can send you more details then.*

Only three of us on board, "the ladies," as the Captain calls us, all congenial. No French on board, as three of the officers are from southeastern Europe, and everybody else is Filipino. Food plentiful and okay, but too salty, too fatty, etc. I suspected this might be a problem, so I don't expect to gain weight!

Hope you made it back home without too much trouble. I was worried about your driving at night in unfamiliar territory. It was so good of you to bring me. Please give everybody a hug for me, especially Tricksy and Pogo. And a big kiss to you.

Please respond to this address so I can be sure you've gotten it.

Love you,
S

The pitching and rolling finally got to me as I was trying to balance through my yoga this morning. I tried changing the direction of the mat

15

from fore-to-aft to starboard-to-port, but that didn't help, and I found myself getting slightly nauseated. At night or in any stationary position, really, the motion of the ship is hardly noticeable. Or, if it is, it's the kind of side-to-side motion that rocks you sweetly to sleep. When I got up from dinner last night, where I'd been perfectly comfortable, a roll caught me by surprise and I reeled drunkenly out of the room, to the great amusement of the officers. Out on deck, I learned long ago to focus on the horizon, and then I'm fine. The comforting old wood and brass inclinometers in all the ship's offices show how close we keep to dead level in the water (closer than it feels!). Cristi explained that the wing-like stabilizers that are extended from the hulls of passenger liners (especially before meals) would slow a freighter down, and speed is all-important in the transport of cargo around the world. I realized with a little shock that the *Louise* had docked, fueled and loaded at one of the busiest ports on the planet in the space of nine short hours!

Day Four, at Sea: Cristi and I had some rare on-deck moments yesterday when the sun came out during the afternoon. She's a snow-bird; like many other Europeans I've met, she can't get enough sun and will sit out on deck by the hour when conditions permit. Living in the tropics as I do, and having once had sun stroke, I limit my exposure to just a few minutes at a time. We're still chasing through some cloudy weather with winds too high to allow Third Mate to take us forward to the lookout at the bow, where somewhere in the Caribbean Cristi and Lila saw a pod of porpoises sporting in the bow wave. Like the birds on board, the porpoises chase the bait fish that are plowed up there. We are traveling with our own little ecosystem.

The Captain sent off my message to Roger yesterday, so I hope sometime today I get a response. If not, I'll try calling again later today.

The Grand Event yesterday was our engine room tour, guided by the voluble Chief Engineer, Karlo. It was one of the most impressive sights any of us had ever seen (although hot and noisy, even with earmuffs). From the keel to the topmost access hatch, it rises 10 stories high, and aft-to-forward takes up 30% of the entire hull – add in the fuel storage tanks along either bulkhead, and it uses up more space than the cargo hold. Lila had the good sense to bring along a notebook, and her jottings added to my memory and a further interview with the Chief, produced some remarkable statistics. The eight-cylinder twin-turbo-charged main engine produces 35,000 horsepower at 91 rpm, and Karlo assured us that newer ships (this one is only nine years old) can produce up to 105,000. To convey the scale of this monster, we saw two new replacement pistons hanging aft of the engine, still wrapped in plastic, each measuring five meters high, and we were told that the 7.5 meter diameter propeller weighs 45 metric tons.

At full speed, the *Louise* burns 110 tons of fuel a day, on "economy speed" 70, at $350 to $400 U.S. per ton. Depending on conditions – currents, depth, wind and weather – it takes an hour and a half to move this fully-loaded ship up to her maximum speed of 23.5 knots per hour. That's a lot of inertia. I didn't ask how long it takes to come to a full stop.

Because bunker fuel is as thick as asphalt, it needs to be purified by means of an on-board centrifuge and then heated to 145C where it becomes viscous enough to be burned. The sludge that remains after purification is pumped into tanker trucks in port. No unprocessed fuel, oil, or bilge contents go into the ocean. (Neither does sewage.) Because of European and West Coast U.S. environmental regulations, in addition to the 3,500 tons of bunker the ship has to carry low-sulphur fuel for use in those ports, as well as gasoline to use dockside. With her tanks topped up, the *Louise* has a range of 15,000 nautical miles.

In addition to the main engine, there are four diesel-run generators, producing 440 volts at 60 cycles for a total potential of six megawatts (newer ships can produce up to 6,600 volts) and a desalinization plant that produces 25 tons of water a day. This multi-staged water-maker, which includes mineralizing and treatment with ultraviolet light, produces all the water used on board for cooling, hydraulics, plumbing and human consumption. The *Louise* takes on no fresh water in port.

Impressive also was the workshop and spare parts storage, including every kind of machine tool, a huge lathe, untold numbers of hand-tools – each in its numbered slot on the walls – shelf after shelf of steel boxes filled with every kind of fitting the ship's engineers could possibly need, paints, chemicals, and numberless drums of oil. As Karlo pointed out, there's no handy machine shop out here in the middle of the Pacific. He described for us, too, all the backed-up back-up systems for running the show, all computerized and far too complicated to recount.

In that vast space amid the hellish din of so many thousands of mechanical parts moving simultaneously at high speeds, surrounded by a labyrinthine complexity of ladders and hatches, kilometers of insulated wires and pipes snaking in every direction, valves, blowers, boilers, turbines, turbo-chargers, condensers, a steering gear the size of two small farm tractors, air compressors, a seawater central cooling system, block-

17

and-tackle for moving heavy equipment around, and a 3,300 volt bow-thruster – with that enormous, panting, thrumming monster-engine at its heart – the steel planks vibrating beneath our feet with the eternal beat of the ship, the three of us stood open-mouthed in awe.

My husband would have loved it.

Today we crossed the Equator, after Lila had sat waiting for an hour and a half on the Bridge, her eyes never straying far from the latitude indicator counting backwards to zero on the broad panel before her. Just as pod after pod of porpoises frolicked alongside, the indicator shifted from N to S, and we were in the Southern Hemisphere. (No red line to mark the spot.) Second Mate gave us each certificates, signed by the Captain, proving we'd done it. We'd all been over it before, by air, land or sea, but none of us had ever been "certified."

Day Five, at Sea: *Maybe this is what my friend was talking about when she said the first week would be difficult. So far it's been a whirlwind of activity. The first time you do anything on board – even laundry – is a new experience, and I've had little opportunity or inclination to brood about some of the things that have brought me here. The pain has even improved; only the first two nights did I need to take something serious to deaden it. I've even been enlivened by fantasies of being attractive to other men – which, since I am the oldest person on board, should be pretty ridiculous. And then I come down with conjunctivitis, probably picked up in Panama, the diarrhea threatens to come back, and I panic. This morning – another time zone passed, so even though I try to stay up later, I'm still awake at the very dark edge of the zone – the pain kicked me out of bed. I've been forgetting to put a couple of acetaminophen on the nightstand to take when I wake in the middle of the night. Another little adjustment. And I think, again, that I'm not fit to be doing this; the discomforts – and the depression – so easily overcome me!*

I tell myself to look at the bright side. Roger was surely right when he said I may never have the opportunity to do something like this again. So I'm doing it, and if it's physically challenging, then please, God, let me treasure the moments when I have them.

And I still can't get through to him. No sat-phone connection yesterday either, and he hasn't responded to my email of two days ago, so I don't even have the assurance that he made it home safely. The Captain wasn't comforting yesterday when he told me that a tropical storm went ashore at Belize two days ago – I know the flooding, landslides, high winds can play havoc with communications all over Central America. Roads too. So I worry. If I don't hear today, I'll try calling my sister up north. We're on the same time zone for once, so I'll know when to call her!

Day Six, at Sea: It feels as if we're zipping through the time zones at mach speed – once a night now, so that every evening after dinner I come up to my cabin and try to read and stay awake until at least nine o'clock – realizing it's really going to be only eight o'clock, which seems ridiculous where I don't have to worry about the monkeys waking me up at 5:00, if our dogs haven't done it earlier. I am still waking up in the dark, and still waking up unsure if I really set the bedside clock back one hour before I turned off the light. So I have to turn on my computer and check the time in Costa Rica, then check the handy little world time-zone map on the wall, and then try to remember how many zones we've passed already. All this activity – up at 5:30 this morning, which really turned out to be 4:30 – makes me starving by the time breakfast is served at 7:00 (or 6:00 . . .), so this morning I went back to bed. Today, Greenwich Mean Time minus nine????

The Captain had the great kindness yesterday, when I still couldn't connect to our home number or to my sister Alison on the sat-phone, to try the number on his own voice-secured direct-to-satellite link on his desk. Both numbers continue to be unavailable. My only option now is to write to Alison.

E-mail to: Alison, by way of the Captain's mail
Hi sweetie,
I'm fine, but I didn't discover till I was on board that I'd have no Internet access except through the Captain's email. I've been trying to reach Roger, and last night you, by way of the satellite-phone, but have not been able to get through.
I sent Roger a note on Monday, courtesy of the Captain, but his habit is to delete mail if he doesn't recognize who it's from.
Could you please call him tonight and ask him to send me a brief note at this address so I know everything there is all right? When we said goodbye late afternoon Friday he was planning to drive as far toward the

border as he could get . . . in the dark. Which has had me worried ever since.

We've crossed the Equator and are still five days out from Tahiti, weather mostly good, I'm writing up a storm. Only porpoises so far! Too bad I didn't take up Serbo-Croatian or Tagalog. More details when I find an Internet café in Papeete.

Love you!

S

Second Mate saved me by finding an antibiotic eye ointment down in the medicines store, and I was almost instantly better . . . and more cheerful. In all the multiple checklists, neither my experienced traveler-friends nor I had thought of an eye infection. Neither, I realized yesterday when Lila mentioned dental work, did a tooth emergency occur to any of us. Imagine having a molar pulled in Fiji!

It has taken several days to figure out who does what on board the *Louise*. No one has thoughtfully posted a list of job descriptions on any of the bulletin boards beyond who's on which emergency response team. Only because he was in charge of the safety orientation did I call Third Mate Denny, who then told me to go to Second Mate Enrique about my eye infection; thus I learned that it's Enrique who has the key to the medicines store down in the infirmary and that, if you want something from there you may have to search all over the ship to find him, since the watches aren't posted for the passengers' convenience either. Only by trial and error have I learned that Denny is on the Bridge in the mornings, when the Captain is also likely to be there, and that Enrique has the afternoon watch (it's his voice we always hear making the p.a. announcements at lunch, which he always terminates with "Good appetite") and that the Captain is always in his office in the afternoons, but if I need anything from the ship's office down on A Deck, I will find First Mate there only in the mornings. Who handles the night watches is anybody's guess.

I'm not sure how much these divisions of labor are common or just specific to the *Louise*. But the importance of a strict hierarchy of command is universal. Nobody quite prepares the passengers to deal with this either. But I had my first hint of its importance when Chief Cook Ernesto was introducing me to the crew members who were at the karaoke party I got shanghaied into. To be polite I asked for everybody's name. Ernesto rushed off to fetch me a crew list, which is not in alphabetical order but in the hierarchical order of the sea, Captain first, Messman last. As Ernesto pointed out who was who and I nodded to each in turn, repeating their first names out loud, he stressed their job titles, including his own, to which I responded, "Chief Cook! I guess I'll have to be nice to you!" And that's what his mates call him, "Chief Cook," and Bosun is always "Bosun." Aside from reinforcing the discipline that any hierarchy demands, the use of titles on board is a gesture of respect and probably – among the lower orders, certainly – a recognition of status. This is why, whenever the Captain is around, I carefully observe the custom and call Chief Engineer "Chief," even though Karlo invited me to use his name from the first day we met. The Captain, of course, is never anything but.

After breakfast yesterday, Cristi and I labored up the stairs and before the last flight my thigh muscles almost completely gave out. I was sorely tempted, but too ashamed in front of her, to take the elevator for only 22 steps (although I would have done it had I been alone!). Sheer muscle fatigue from trying to pedal that exercise bike down in the gym. I decided today to just do yoga and give my poor legs a break. It turned out to be a bad pain day anyway – who knows why? – so I stayed in my cabin writing or just lying down listening to music. I'm so glad I thought to load some favorites into the computer before I left, although yesterday I borrowed two CDs from the Officers' Lounge, selections of arias sung by Pavarotti and Domingo. I remember that in their heyday I used to maintain that Domingo was the better of the two. Now, with a more mature understanding of the purity of his tone and his exquisite phrasing, I know Pavarotti is the clear winner. What a pleasure to just listen. I wonder why I almost never do this at home?

The evening's entertainment has now settled down to a pre-dinner drink in the Officers' Lounge with Chief Engineer Karlo presiding behind the bar and he and the Captain swapping lively stories about the sea and ships while electrician Igor hulks wordlessly over his beer. If I could remember the half of what we hear before dinner, I'd have a much longer book to write!

I enlisted Karlo's help in making sure that what I had written about the engine room and the ship's complicated systems was accurate. He was kind enough to check my draft, make corrections and even suggest some additions, which we went over before the Captain joined us yesterday evening. Everyone has shown such a willingness to be helpful, but I wonder: last night after dinner, I said goodnight to Lila and Cristi as they were going into the Officers' Lounge for a cigarette, and I noticed that the electrician had changed all the plastic light covers from their usual opaque white to red and blue. Does he imagine that these colors over the ceiling fluorescents are more conducive to a party atmosphere?

There is the sweet smell of salt on the air. And, with the moon not yet risen, there is a foreign country of constellations in the sky.

A return email from my sister today; the Captain left it at my place at lunch. They've called Roger in Costa Rica. What a relief to know all is well! It's so strange how just a few days and a few kilometers of ocean can make one feel so far away from family and home. I wanted to read her brief message again and again, my first tangible connection since I've been away.

Day Seven, at Sea: I woke early and pulled the curtain back from the porthole in time to see the sky just pearling up before sunrise. I quickly dressed and climbed to my usual perch on the top step to F Deck, facing aft, a little northeasterly. It was slow in coming. First a faint pink lined the clouds, then a golden light gradually deepened along the horizon, and puffs of cloud over the indigo water turned from mauve, to rose, to bright pink. The horizon clouds opened to form a rose-tinged bowl, scalloped like a seashell, and suddenly the sunlight poured into this bowl like molten gold, too brilliant to look at. I watched for half an hour, at the end of which I fully felt the blessing of this diurnal gift to the planet.

Although the prospect was a little frightening at first, I haven't minded being out of sight of land. Not only have we seen no land, except for our little on-board colony of birds and the porpoises on the Equator, we have seen no other living thing. Not even a ship on the horizon, which seems strange, as these shipping lanes must be well-traveled. Except for the myriad invisible life-forms beneath the sea, we are utterly alone out here, and I am not bothered by this a bit. Perhaps, living closed up in cities as so many people do, they miss an appreciation of the sheer grandness of the planet around us. How many times did I see a rainbow from a city street? I was lucky to have received a friendly impression of the universe when I was young. Infinite sky, infinite stars, infinite sea. Now, as I grow old, I'm grateful that infinity is not such a daunting idea.

It seems that every time the Captain or the Chief Engineer speaks, I want to start taking notes. It's wonderful to be learning so much about the ship. Last evening, I even learned that the overall magnetic polarity of a steel ship depends on which hemisphere it is built in. What a mind-bending idea! The Captain was telling me about both the compasses on board, an electric gyro compass on the Bridge that spins at 35,000 revolutions per minute, and up above – on "monkey deck," where he will take us only in calm weather – is the magnetic compass, which requires no other energy to run. He was Master of a ship once that was struck by lightning in the open sea. Three times in instant succession, tens of thousands of volts struck the radio antenna and knocked it to the deck, where it grounded on the hull. All the electronics on the Bridge were fried, and he had to bring the ship into port the old way, using a sextant, the sun, moon and stars and the horizon – just as his seaman ancestors did hundreds of years ago. He said young mariner trainees aren't learning these old skills with the same rigor earlier generations did. "Why do we need it?" they ask, "when we can know our position anywhere in the world instantly by satellite?" There was a fierce conviction in his look as the Captain next said, "One thermonuclear explosion would disrupt the Earth's magnetic field enough to knock out satellite communications everywhere on the planet." A chilling thought.

My diet is completely shot. There's aspartame in the yogurt, high-fructose corn syrup in the breakfast juice, butter all over the vegetables, ground beef lurking in the tomato sauce, sausage bobbing in the lentil soup. I will have to wait till next year to get my cholesterol checked.

Not remembering my nautical terms too well, I asked the Captain to remind me of the difference between pitching and rolling. His explanation: if the waves are coming on the bow, the ship will pitch, that is, she will sink down nose-first into the trough of the wave and then climb back up. If the waves are on the beam (sideways), the ship will roll, that is tilt side to side like an old Seth Thomas metronome. If the waves are on the stern quarter, that is, not directly on the stern but coming from slightly port or starboard, as now, the ship is *yawing,* which means a combination of pitching *and* rolling. If you can imagine a bulk like the *Louise* doing a three-quarters wiggle between a roll and pitch, you've got it.

23

The Captain explains that these stern-quarter waves are radiating out from a huge storm off southern Argentina, 3,000 miles away, and I have to wonder how big they were to start with!

Sun Salutation (Hatha Yoga More-or-Less): Begin with Mountain Pose, planting feet firmly about half the width of the yoga mat apart for balance, arms at your sides. Feel your core gyrating with the motion of the ship. Breathe deeply as you reach skywards and join your hands above your head, leaning gently back. Use left hand against the bulkhead for support. Bending at the hips, drop your head to your knees, palms touching the floor on either side of your feet. Skip to the right. Look forward briefly, but not at the tilting horizon. Shift your feet carefully back until you are in the Plank Position – you will have no limbs free for this operation, so quickly raise your upper body on your extended arms and hold Upward Facing Dog for a count of five. Keep your right arm ready to fend off the coffee table. Drop your head to the floor then raise your hips into Downward Facing Dog. Turn your feet inwards as much as necessary to hold this position, flex knees only if you have to, for a count of five. Breathe. You want to feel that long stretch of the hamstrings. Return to front of mat, bend at the hips, hands on the floor. Skip to the left. Raise your upper body and join your hands above your head, arching your back, as before. Lurch forward. Stagger back. Do-si-do.

The sunlight streaming through the patchy clouds turns the surface of the sea to beaten silver.

Day Eight, At Sea: Another time zone flitted past last night. Now we're at GMT minus ten. Only two more zones to cross before it will be the day before.

The Captain enjoys complete authority over the ship and crew, and he seems to truly enjoy the role – which means he doesn't always conform to my idea of interpersonal courtesy when he's giving orders. He believes in running a tight ship, a good thing since we all depend utterly on his judgment and expertise. But, he's also one of the funniest men I've ever met. He's a big man who favors knee-length pants, voluminous shirts, gold chains and shoes without socks, and he sports a crew-cut and Van Dyke – all this not at all what I was expecting in the Master of a ship. But I find I like him – he's sincere, vastly knowledgeable and gregarious. Last evening before dinner I was alone in the Lounge, when he came in and said, "Where is the bartender? Where is the entertainment?" It had been a difficult afternoon for me, and I was wondering the same thing, not feeling up to making amusing small-talk. But I did ask him if he had his own boat, and by the time he'd described it and what he does with it (fish principally, but also occasionally engage in other activities that he prefers his wife remain ignorant of), the others had shown up and he'd steamed into a fantastic story that had all of us doubled over with laughter. It wouldn't be fair of me to tell it, even though his wife knows about it, but Cristi and I have been giggling every time we run into each other today over key words and phrases like: "Something's really burning."; "Look Mami, Papi's on TV!"; and the past-tense verb "zoom-éd."

Seating at meals is rigidly established, and no one varies from his place. There are two tables, a rectangular one to accommodate six officers, headed by the Captain, and a round one for four passengers, where Cristi, Lila and I sit, always in the same places. Joining the Captain are the Chief Engineer and the electrician (technically not an officer but, since he speaks no language common to the rest of the crew, is permitted the privilege), both sitting to the Captain's right (in that order) and thus facing the small round table for four. The Filipino officers, First, Second and Third Mates, do not take advantage of their places at the Captain's table, but seem to prefer to eat in the Crew's Mess. This means there is no one seated with their backs to us at the Captain's table, and it feels as if we are eating for an audience. This, sad to say, makes me feel somewhat self-conscious, so I find myself eating very slowly and, it turns out, very little, because I'm losing weight. It certainly would never occur to anyone to invite anybody else – us, for example – to fill those three empty places at the head table.

I find not only my self-consciousness disturbing, but also the fact that there is not any even quasi-social fraternization between the Balkan and the Filipino officers. The latter never come into the Lounge, and I several times have met two of them in the Crew's Recreation room at the opposite side of the ship (where the karaoke music is ear-splitting). So all of this will be interesting tonight, when we have a "barbecue party" in the stern, where there will be only one long table to accommodate everybody.

Day Nine, at Sea: I wrote some emails this morning, which I put on a flash-drive to take to an Internet café when we hit port.

Email to: *Alison:*

Thanks, dear heart, for your note letting me know all was okay. It was my first contact with home, and I read it over and over. In Papeete now and loving this voyage, although I've had some painful times as I try to get used to a different physical environment. I still haven't heard from Roger, so I've been trying not to worry. You said he had a bug – is he very sick? Mad? Or just not wanting to bother me? It's amazing how, after so many years together, I still can't read him. I'll write him again today.

There have been moments on this journey when I've just wanted to weep, but so far have not allowed myself the luxury of completely letting go. When you have to show up three times a day for meals, you tend to discipline yourself more, I think. It's a small community on board, just 19 crew and 3 passengers, only 6 of us in the Officers' Mess.

Mostly glorious weather . . . but you'll read all the details in my lengthy journal, sent under separate mail.

Love you, S

The barbecue party was the first occasion to go to the main deck since coming aboard, when I was whisked above to my cabin so quickly I hardly saw anything. It's a working deck, nothing you'd care to stumble around in on a dark night, long alleys along either side of the ship leading from the bow aft to the poop deck (which calls to mind be-wigged captains in tricorns striding back and forth tongue-lashing their officers). The vast space was roofed with the undersides of containers, the reefers dripping condensation on the long common table. The poor lighting away from the table made everything appear a uniform black against the nighttime sea, only the pipes and fittings standing out in stark red, yellow or white. Lurking in the shadows were a number of giant winches wrapped with two-inch-thick steel-core mooring lines, and bollards popped up randomly like iron mushrooms. There were steel cages to starboard and port to protect line handlers from a snapped cable. And they do snap, the Captain assured me; loaded, the ship weighs 45,000 tons. To starboard Cook had set up a huge gas grill, and the smoke added to the general murkiness of the atmosphere. (At one point the Captain leaned over to me and said, "You won't find this ambience in any restaurant on land!" Indeed.) Next to the grill stood a table filled with large trays of beef, pork, lamb, cuttlefish, squid and shrimp. All of these were delivered cooked to the center of the eating table, along with great buckets of salads, pastas and garlic bread.

The seating was predictable, with the Chief Engineer and electrician to the right of the head of the table, and we passengers on the left. We were seated on chairs from the Mess, while the Filipino end of the table made do with wooden benches. There seemed to be goodwill all around, notwithstanding this arrangement, and we all applauded enthusiastically when Cook made an appearance at the table.

The throbbing of the giant propeller just under our feet would have made conversation impossible enough without the blaring pop music coming from the sound system set up by the crew. To be heard, you had to lean in to your neighbor's ear. Which Lila did at one point, saying to me, "Go back to the stern." Unsteadily, I made my way aft and I was grateful to be able to grab onto a bulwark because the sight of the ship's wake was vertiginous: a massive, churning trail of white water from starboard to port and stretching into black infinity. From above, where I've been living for the past week, the ship doesn't seem to be moving very fast; in fact, I would have described her progress as *stately*. But, from the taffrail, which I clung to with arms held stiffly in front of me, it felt faster than a speedboat.

We held on until the karaoke microphone appeared, which is when we said good-night to everyone and climbed back up to the quiet of our rooms. I stepped outside for one last look at the night sky and saw the Big Dipper tilted on the northern horizon. Somewhere gleams the Southern Cross in the faraway, crystalline dark.

The three passengers gathered in the E Deck lounge after dinner and talked about places to come, especially Australia, where Cristi has already been three times. Unfortunately, we will not be sailing past the Sydney Opera House, because the ship's draft will be too deep for the channel under the Harbour Bridge, so we'll be docking at Botany Bay instead. If there's a way to get to the Underground near there, I'll let Cristi lead me to a stop near the Opera House. Otherwise, we'll have to find a taxi to the airport and take the Underground from there. I would be so disappointed to miss it!

Day Ten, at Sea: I have been settling into a routine – although any little event can upset it. On the wide ocean, novelty always wins. If I'm up long before breakfast, I work at the computer a bit, going over what's been written before, or making notes on new material. If the weather's fine – which it has been lately – I go topside to watch the sunrise. Today's was glorious, a triple-decker, three separate appearances of the white-hot sun before it had cleared the clouds. Breakfast with Cristi at seven. (Lila usually sleeps in.) Then back to my cabin for some more time on the computer until my breakfast has settled, when I do yoga and then clatter down to the gym for my punishing workout (along with the rowing machine stashed in a corner of the gym, I've discovered a whole new set of muscles in my back). By the time I've finished, Manny, the Messman/Steward, has usually cleaned the cabin, so I change and go up to join Cristi on deck, where I sit in the sun for 15 minutes or so and then get in under the shade of the Bridge-wing to watch the ocean happen. We watch the white-caps rolling by or the birds hunting the wave-tops; so far there hasn't been much more to see. Cristi and I can be companionably quiet together, and only every once in a while does either of us feel the need to say anything. Usually around ten the tantalizing smell of sautéing garlic or onions wafts up to F Deck from the Galley vents, and one of us always says, "Cook's making lunch!" After an hour or so on deck, I've had enough glare (it's noticeably brighter at sea than inland) and computer work follows, writing or downloading photos, which lasts until noon. At any time during this routine, if I need a stretch I go out on deck, or if I need a quick lie-down I take it.

Lunch is served at noon, when Lila and the officers show up, after which I usually spend the afternoon listening to music or reading . . . trying to stay off the computer. I had promised myself to work regularly on French, but have only done that twice so far. I justify my laziness with the excuse that both my shipmates have some French, too, and I figure that in Papeete among the three of us we should be able to come up with a complete sentence if we have to! By 5:15 I've showered and put on warmer clothes for the frigid conditions down on B Deck and I descend to join the others in the Officers' Mess before dinner, after which I generally don't tarry long. The sea air is wonderfully conducive to sleep, and I read a little before bed. So far I haven't been bored.

Yesterday's grand interruption in all this was a trip to the bow, accompanied by Denny, the Third Mate. If the stern is all about power, the bow is pure peace. Standing out there in the tiny lookout, the whole ship behind you, only the endless ocean in front of you, you hear nothing but the sibilant plash of water parting around the hull and the silky breeze brushing past your ears. After the inferno of noise and clamor that is the giant mechanical beast behind you, the bow is as close to pure, heavenly silence as you will get. None of us wanted to leave.

Facing forward at the bow, you can see nothing of the ship except the bulbous bow, green with algae, pushing through the clear water three stories down. With no point of reference, it looks much closer, just under your feet. We had been told that the hollow bulbous bow – which looks like a disfigurement on the otherwise clean cutting-edge of a ship's prow – creates a vacuum and sucks water in behind it which makes the vessel . . . can I say, more "hydrodynamic?"

While waiting for the others to take pictures, Denny and I chatted for a bit in the shade of one of the winches. He told me he comes from a long line of what he calls "seafarers." What a lovely word! *Seaman* is a working word, a classification, a job description. In order to handle the helm, you have to have the education and experience to reach the level of "able seaman," for instance. An every-day, practical word that carries none of the romance or tradition of exploration and discovery, none of the love of the sea that *seafarer* does. Denny said he finds peace at sea; he says it's clean; it's in his blood. I can understand that.

I complimented Cook on the dipping sauce for the shrimp that was served only at the Filipino end of the barbecue party table. When I asked some of the crew if I could try it, they grinned and handed me a saucer to spoon some into. They probably thought I couldn't take the heat. Today I asked Cook if I could have the recipe. In true chef fashion, he held out the secret ingredient until I pressed him for it – I had both seen and tasted the little red bits of hot stuff in the bottom of the saucer, so I knew it was there! Sambal. "You can get it anywhere," Ernesto scoffed. "Not where I live you can't," said I. Very graciously, he presented me with a jar.

In calmer seas, the ship settles into a more rhythmic roll. I've been playing barcaroles in my head.

This morning Cristi spotted land way off our port bow, a tiny white atoll, barely an azure smudge on the horizon. We climbed up to the bridge to borrow the binoculars. Third Mate showed us the chart – Tikey, one of the Islands of Disappointment! – and then he walked the dividers along our route to estimate the hours at which we should see more. Our first South Pacific Island. Tomorrow Tahiti!

Passage Two
Tahiti to Fiji
Time Travel, Heart Travail

Day Eleven, Tahiti: *I spent a bad night, having taken an anti-inflammatory in the late afternoon to try to ease the pain at the base of my neck. Just as I got up from the dinner table I was hit with a cramp that almost doubled me over, the most severe I've experienced in a long time. In my cabin, having taken everything I had that might help me get over it, I was struck with all kinds of dire fantasies – colon cancer, burst gallbladder, peritonitis. Then I saw myself in a Tahitian hospital, attended by caring French Nursing Sisters, and unable to express a word of what I was suffering. (If I carry these fantasies far enough, sometimes they make me laugh.)*

One of the first thoughts, of course, is that I am in no way fit for this trip. I shouldn't have come. I shouldn't have spent all this money, when our financial future is so uncertain. I shouldn't have been so selfish.

Another thought, which reminds me of my grandmother, Leora, is that my body is punishing me for thinking it could still be attractive to other people. Fantasy, I realized, at least at the yearning schoolgirl level, is nothing more than an interpretation of other people's behavior in terms of our own desires, and is ultimately egocentric. It can be fun, as long as you don't take it too seriously, as long as you don't flip to the dark side of "I'll never be enough."

Pain is the final "I'll never be enough" for me. And not just pain, but age, disfigurement, physical limitations and all those related demons. Obviously, putting my self-esteem at the mercy of my body at this age is Not a Good Idea!

31

I woke to the thump-thump of the ship's engine at low speed as she steamed into Papeete Harbor, made a couple of sharp left turns and lined herself up to be nudged gently to the dock by an efficient tugboat. The sky was turning pre-dawn pearly, just enough light to see the famous headland we've all been impressed by in the Bounty movies. Lights made a cheery sight along the shore and stretching up into the hills. Once we were tied down to the dock, the day came on quietly, gently. A couple of outrigger canoes were plying their way across the still black water of the harbor, rippling the mirror image of the massive green hulk of the headland.

Once beyond the development along the waterfront, Tahiti looks much like parts of Costa Rica – virtually the same vegetation, but without the snakes. There were even a few street mutts that could have been imported from the Costa Rican gene pool, including one right down on the dock in the middle of all the hullabaloo of unloading and loading containers.

The Captain had arranged for us to be met by an English-speaking Chinese Tahitian lady with an air-conditioned van. She took us on a two-hour tour along the north coast of the island to see a spectacular inland waterfall and to visit the monuments to Captain Cook and the H.M.S. Bounty, and the Point Venus lighthouse, all in a lovely beach-side park. The water was calm and so inviting! Along the way we spotted long tubular "mail boxes" mounted on posts at the roadside. Emilie tried to get us to guess what they were for, but after newspapers and banana leaves we could come up with nothing. Delighted, Emilie cried, "Baguettes, of course!"

At another lovely beach, I saw a young French woman weaving pretty baskets out of palm fronds. I almost walked past her, but she caught me with "Where are you from?" in almost un-accented English. When I told her Costa Rica, she said she was envious and she asked about yoga centers and opportunities there for alternative life-styles (whatever that means), and so we chatted while the others went on to look at a sea spout at the end of the rocks. I found it ironic that this pretty, well-spoken young woman, sitting in the shade of some palm trees on a postcard-perfect Tahitian beach was telling me she wished she were in Costa Rica! I bought one of her smallest baskets in compensation.

After the tour, Emilie dropped us off at a jeweler's, where Lila was intent on buying a black pearl necklace, and Cristi and I drifted down the street to a very nice outdoor café where we ate lunch – Polynesian-style raw fish marinated in coconut milk. Lila joined us and we went around the corner to the Internet café . . . where the keyboard was in French, and I couldn't copy and paste my distribution list into the mail I had wanted to send to everyone with my promised "log" about the adventure so far. I quickly answered a few mails, as briefly as possible since I had to type everything twice, and was at least able to attach the log to these few. But in future the only answer for this will be taking my own computer – where the letters are in their accustomed places! – to a café. It was frustrating, not to mention hot in the tiny upstairs café, and half an hour cost me almost $5, so I gave up. Let's hope I have better luck in Fiji.

Lila and Cristi were happy to continue exploring in town, but I had had enough, and I found the taxi stand and managed in my mangled French to tell the driver where I wanted to go. There was quite a long walk from the security gate to the ship, container-moving vehicles of all kinds trundling this way and that, zipping unexpectedly out of alleys between container stacks, no safe walkway for the odd pedestrian passenger, and I felt very much at risk of being obliterated. There seems to be no one on the ground coordinating all this motion.

I was alone at the dinner table, but since we'd reached a new culinary nadir – macaroni and cheese – I didn't stay long, and I came up to my cabin to listen to music and read. The booms and bangs and ship-shudderings of the loading and unloading went on long after I went to bed, feeling the day had been a bit of a test for me with all the walking, and that, frustrations or no, I felt satisfied at my ability to do that much.

The fact that I still haven't heard from Roger makes me want to cry or pound on the table in fury or both. It was over a week ago that I wrote him to find out how he was and give him the Captain's email address so he could let me know. Then Alison was in touch with him, urging him to write, but nothing in all this time, either through the Captain's mail or my own.

I don't know how to interpret this behavior. He wants to leave me alone? He doesn't want to bother me with details of home? He's subconsciously angry at me for leaving? He's just being a jerk? No matter how I poke through all these possibilities, I end up stymied. Last night before bed, I said to myself (assuming even the most positive guess about his behavior), "How can I be married to a man who can't communicate?"

Day Twelve, Tahiti: Our second opportunity to visit Papeete was delayed an hour because no one was sure when we would have to be back. Finally, a little after 9:30 the word came down telling us to be on board again no later than 1:00. Lila and I charged off to the gate on foot, and then begged

33

the kindness of one of the security guards to call us a taxi. We had been spoiled by Emilie – now we had to use our French, although the extremely fat woman driving the mini-Peugeot had a few words of English. Fortunately, Lila is quicker with her French than I am, so we made it into the center of town with no problem. Trickier was my attempt to explain to the driver that I hoped she could wait for me while I changed money at the bank (more paperwork than in Costa Rica!), then take me to the beach we had visited the day before, wait for me there while I swam and then bring me back to town to meet Lila in time for a quick lunch. I also wanted to stop at a store and pick up a couple of things to donate to the Officers' Mess. Somehow, the two of us, trying hard, managed to understand each other and at the end of all that I expostulated, *"Ma Francais est horrible!"*

"Oui," she laughed, *"horrible."*

She took me out to Point Venus where I was able to change in the rest room while she parked the taxi in the shade. Not wanting to leave anything valuable on the beach, I trusted her with my purse. Point Venus is a black-sand beach and well shaded by what look like casuarina trees, so the sand is cool and there's no glare close in to shore, where I swam. Cool salt water. It was heaven to float there, gazing over at that magnificent mist-draped headland, the cumulus clouds on the horizon piled up as dense as cotton-wool, and my aging body painless for the first time in almost two weeks.

I was only ten minutes late meeting Lila, but after the supermarket I was a little short for the taxi fare, and the banks close in Papeete at 11:30! Lila lent me the money and we went to a brasserie on the main avenue overlooking the cruise ship dock. In the two relatively upscale restaurants where I have lunched in Papeete, all the clientele is French, with only a few tourists. And the menus tend to be heavy. My *salade césar* came in a huge bowl with sliced hard-cooked egg and a load of fatty little hunks of ham. The dark greens, however, were a treat after the iceberg lettuce served on board (iceberg keeps longer). The bread, too, was a major improvement. And the beer – brewed right there – was better than anything in Costa Rica.

We made it back on board with five minutes to spare. This time the taxi driver spoke fluent English, learned over many years at sea working for a Norwegian line. "Name a place," he said, "and I've been there." I don't know why it occurred to me to say "Vladivostok," but he said that was one place he hadn't been.

It seems that a lot of islanders go to sea. It amazes me that, for millennia before the arrival of those who claimed to discover these islands, the people here had the courage to shove off in their primitive canoes or rafts and sail beyond the horizon, while for centuries Europeans were afraid of falling off the edge of the world.

Things can be expensive in Papeete. This is probably true of most places where cruise ships dock, but even more so on an island where everything has to be imported over great distances and through multiple agencies before reaching the stores. Both lunches cost me more than $20 and I paid $7.50 for a four-day-old International Herald Tribune!

An hour or so after we were back on board, Lila knocked on my door to tell me there was a wi-fi signal on the bridge. I grabbed my computer and ran up the two flights of stairs, where I discovered the battery was almost dead. Downstairs again to get the adapters and cables. Upstairs I found I didn't have the flash drive I'd been wearing around my neck all morning with the emails I hadn't managed to send on it. Back downstairs I went, rooted around in my purse until I finally found it, then dashed back to the bridge with the urgency of fear that we would be leaving port at any moment. Plenty of exercise! As it happened, I picked up several stray signals and had enough time to download software updates as well as catch up on mail. First Mate and Lila were both availing themselves of the rare opportunity too. We arrived in port at dawn yesterday and one supposes the Internet connection has been available ever since. I wonder why nobody told us before?

Late in the afternoon, I was sitting in the lounge when I felt a rumble in the belly of the ship; our giant propeller had begun to turn and suddenly the containers on shore were slipping past the porthole. I stepped out on deck to watch our progress out of the harbor. There were pilot tugs on either side guiding us through the tight turns and into the channel in the fading light. There was a rainbow over the magnificent headland of Tahiti. The Point Venus lighthouse flashed like a star near the horizon, and the strange Polynesian twin-hulled barge we had seen tied up on the far side of the port – seemingly made of wood and with two high, red, gaff-rigged sails – plowed soundlessly off to starboard. We cleared the harbor entrance just as the sun sank into the ocean; our tugs turned back. We were once again at sea. A surge of joy lifted my heart.

There are three cranes on this ship, two forward and one aft. (Off Panama, I saw more than one ship with as many as four cranes forward and two aft.) The only ports on this run where the cranes are used are in Tahiti, Fiji and New Caledonia, where the local loading facilities are more primitive. In the more developed ports, ships use the port's shore gantries, in spite of the cost. If the ship can unload and load in a quarter of the time, she can get away from the dock and move her cargo on to the next port a lot faster, so the gantries are more efficient.

Unloading and loading 650 containers in Tahiti took two full days and part of the first night in port. Although there are now a few mobile cranes on the dock, we used the ship's cranes. (Even so, the crane operators are employees of the port.) I'm assuming the cost to hire the port's cranes doesn't figure in the bean-counters' estimates for this leg of the journey, but we were forced to use one of the hired cranes because our own number-two crane was out of service. The Captain has to make these kinds of decisions on the spot . . . and he takes the heat from the Head Office when he has to incur cost overruns.

I think this is what happened yesterday because the Captain seemed to be at flash-point all day. Added to his apparent frustration about the crane was the fact that he had been planning to go deep-water diving in the morning on an old World War Two wreck that he hadn't seen before. When I saw him on the bridge in the afternoon, I learned that our malfunctioning crane had forced him to stay with the ship, and he was more than a little annoyed.

Also annoying, no doubt, was the dock workers' *tortuguismo*, that wonderful Costa Rican expression for behaving like turtles, that is, in slow motion. The Captain has no patience with French ports in general, and with Polynesian port workers in particular. He told me that they had promised to finish up by two o'clock, working straight through their normal break, but instead they all quit at 11:30 and didn't come back until after 1:00.

Finally, at dinner he headed the officers' table all by himself. We had gotten under way at 5:00, and the Chief Engineer and electrician both had to work through the usual dinner hour. He knew this, but we could see he was becoming increasingly agitated. Suddenly he pushed himself up from the table and strode towards the Galley, arms flung up and out in that universal gesture of I've-had-enough, and yelled, "Where are my officers?" This outburst probably embarrassed him, because he disappeared into the Galley and we saw him no more.

Day Thirteen, at Sea: It's a small community on board, 19 officers and crew and three passengers. It's inevitable that those of us in most frequent contact should get to know each other in ways people on passenger cruises rarely do. Not to mention the time factor; I've been on board now for two weeks. That amount of time at close quarters and you start to pick up the subtleties of the relationships around you, as well as feel more at ease with those you find congenial.

Some of the crew I've barely met to say hello to as they pass me in the passageways on their way to their various shifts. Those in the engine room working nights I never see at all. And it's apparent their shifts change; for the first few days we saw a lot of Second Mate, for example. Now I suspect he's up on the bridge at nighttime, because we're seeing more of First Mate now. The European officers work a daylight shift, unless there's something important going on, such as transiting the Canal, or dealing with recalcitrant cranes. For the Canal passage, the Captain was on the bridge for 24 hours straight.

It seems to be true that a full day at sea puts everyone into better spirits. Ports are hard work and obviously stressful – the coordination that has to happen! The shippers have to have their containers in port, the trucks and loaders have to be there to move them on the ground, the cranes have to be working, the port agent has to sign off on each cargo, the containers all have to be accounted for – what goes on, what goes off, which containers are empty and which are full – and full of what – and who's paying for each. There's offloading sludge to be taken care of as well as the topping up the fuel tanks. And then there is the potential for accidents. With all those vehicles moving around on the dock, the crane operators swinging their loads back and forth, workers down below and on deck guiding each container into position . . . it's easy to see how somebody could get squashed.

So it's very soon apparent that everyone in this ship's hierarchy has his job to do, and he has to work as a member of a tight-knit team. My impression so far is that they do work well together, in spite of the prejudices on both sides of the cultural divide. The training every one of them has had in order to qualify for his job, the apprenticeships they all must serve at sea, and the years they've worked, have made all of them professionals, and I'm sure it's mutual respect for all that, as well as a strong dose of professional pride, that keeps the team functioning so well.

Last evening before dinner, when the usual jollity again prevailed in the lounge, I asked the Captain more specifically about the cost of dockage. When my father was pottering around on small yachts, marinas charged per linear foot of hull. That bought you electricity and fresh water and the use of the facilities (showers mainly). Fuel, of course, was extra (although a lot cheaper then!), and you tanked up at a separate dock. The dockage at some marinas in those days was so cheap that a lot of boat owners would leave their boats tied up for a season or more.

In the international shipping business the transport company pays dockage per container moved from the deck to the dock and vice versa. There are different charges for empties, fulls, 20-footers and 40 footers, and probably separate tariffs for "super-heavies," "super-highs" and "reefers" (refrigerated) On average, the Captain said, a typical dockage in a modern port can run a ship this size between $210,000 and $230,000. In those ports use of the gantries is mandatory – they slide on tracks along the docks, nothing could be allowed to get in their way. (The newest ships don't even have cranes.) It's hard to imagine the sheer scale of the economics of international shipping. If it costs that much just to dock, what must the companies be charging for the freight?

At breakfast the other morning, Cristi wondered where the grapefruit had come from. From where I was sitting, I could see there was a label on the one that was still waiting for Lila on the other side of the table. I asked Cristi to pass it to me so I could read it (I am usually the only one of us to have her reading glasses with her). It said "California Red." According to Cristi, the last place we provisioned was in Savannah. At the moment, we were in Tahiti, which meant that the grapefruit had traveled from California to the East Coast (probably not directly to Savannah) and then, in the ship's cooler, all the way down the Eastern Seaboard, through the Panama Canal and a third of the way across the Pacific. When you think about the fuel required for the ocean transport of exported goods, be sure to include the fuel needed to run all those tractor trailers and other vehicles that move the containers around on the docks, and don't forget the fuel for the locomotives or the trucks that bring the containers from the farms and factories to the ports to begin with. It is truly impossible for me to imagine how much that grapefruit cost, although I bet somebody could put a number on it.

Day Fourteen, at Sea: I wondered who had set the exercise machine to forty kilos; nobody on board looked hefty enough to do it, except for the

Captain and, somehow, I knew it wasn't him. It turns out to be Ernesto, Chief Cook. Behind that apron lurks a strong man. All that running around in Papeete had given me a shin splint and made my knees sore, so I was planning to do only a light workout this morning, after three days of nothing at all. When I opened the door to the gym, there was Ernesto, elbows bent over his head, lifting an 18-kilo barbell up and down along his back and going, "Hwoosh, hwoosh." He was a little disconcerted to see me, and I was worried I might be in his way, but we got past that initial discomfort and I mounted the bike and started to plod along. Having him there working so hard pushed me to work a little harder, nine minutes on the bike, and then I did another four or so on the rowing machine, and when Ernesto saw me checking the weight on the big machine, he kindly changed it back to the minimum 10 kilos. A few minutes more on the bike, and I had done all I could. He had noted my time. "Twenty, thirty minutes good," he said.

As I was picking up my things to go, I complimented him directly on the chicken curry he'd made the other night. He admitted there had been sambal in it – I could see as much – and he said he'd tried to make it not too hot so that everybody could enjoy it. Both Lila and I had eaten it, and it was just a tad below our limit of tolerance, but I didn't tell Ernesto that. If he thinks it was mild, fine; we'll see what else he comes up with. He said, "You know you can add chopped garlic to that sauce." He meant the sauce he had served at the barbecue that he'd given me the recipe for. "And it goes good with rice and everything."

"What do you call that sauce, Ernesto?"

"Sweet and sour sauce," he said. It was nothing like any "sweet and sour" sauce I ever ate. Must be that in the Philippines "sweet and sour" is a different animal altogether.

Back out at sea the slight acrophobia I first experienced when I got on board is gone again. Looking out over the railing on E Deck is like staring at the street seven stories below. The rail seems flimsy, and it comes only up to my waist. Send along a sudden big wave, and one could easily unbalance and topple over. Out at sea, though, this fear disappeared. In the open ocean there are no other objects to give you a sense of relative height. The sea seems to come up to meet you; it's only when we see a bird skimming the waves down below that we realize it's so tiny because so far away! At the dock, there are plenty of reminders. The workers look like little toy men, the vehicles Matchbox versions, and even the Captain, standing there talking with the port agent, looks diminutive. Then I find this height alarming, and I stand well back from the rail with at least part of my body in contact with the bulkhead. It's a pleasure to go to sea again and leave this little fear behind.

Day Sixteen, at Sea: Day Fifteen got swallowed up by the International Date Line. No matter, I'll get it back before we dock in New Zealand. And one day out here is very much like another. The only change was that, in the absence of Saturday, the Slop Chest orders were filled on Friday. Don't ask me why they call the ship's store (toothpaste, cigarettes, etc.) the Slop Chest. Not many options there – I bought some Pringles for the Officers' Lounge. (Pringles!!!!)

Full-time physical pain is not conducive to positive thinking, although I think I'm making an effort. I try to be social, to make conversation, to have a witty comeback ready for the Captain's jokes, to listen with attention to the details of Lila's many stressors. Otherwise, except for a brief sunning on the observation deck, I spend my time in my cabin. (The smoke usually chases me out of the E Deck lounge.) I also make a mighty effort not to think about Roger, because every time I do I want to cry. Surely, if he'd cared, he would have found some way to get a message to me. He's not this dumb! I mean, not so dumb as to fail to realize that it's important to me to hear from him. Alison has surely told him I've been upset. We have houseguests keeping Roger company while I'm gone, and I know that at least one of them got my email, and she would certainly have told him I wanted to hear from him. So this, along with the pain, is casting a pall over this trip for me, and last night the thought flitted through my head to fly back from Sydney. There are only two things stopping me: spending the extra money, when I have no way of knowing what our finances are, and a certain ego-pride that doesn't want me to look like a quitter.

While I've had some good insights so far, now only two weeks into this journey, not even half-way, I have hardly found the peace I was seeking. What was that, I wonder? What magic did I think would wipe out all my physical and mental suffering?

Remembering what my friend told me: "Keep looking inward and see what the moment has to teach you," I feel so damned inadequate to whatever task this is!

On the other hand, why do I want to hear from Roger? Isn't this just more wanting from him what I can't get? Isn't this just another way of torturing myself for not being loved enough, wanted enough, cherished enough . . . just not being *enough? The dictum,* be the love you want, *sounds simple, but nothing could be more difficult.*

We go through our married life like ships passing, like roommates, trying to be considerate of each other, each doing our "share" around the house, fulfilling our own commitments to the outside world, dealing with the day-to-day, taking on a bit more if the other isn't feeling well, I usually upstairs, he down in what I call his hidey-hole, his office, where he doesn't want me to enter, where he makes it so obvious every time I do that I am intruding on his private space, and this hurts me every time. What am I? Some monster? His mother?

When I try to talk to him about our marriage, he just freezes. He holds my hand when we watch a movie. He remembers once or twice a year to bring me flowers.

"Do you want to be divorced?" I asked him recently.

"No."

"Why not?"

"I like being around you."

What makes this worse is that we used to share intimate conversations, we used to go out, we danced, we made love. What changed? What am I to do with all this except weep? There are times when I think, okay, being together is at least better than being alone. But frequently I'm not so sure even of that. This is one of the real "whys" behind this voyage. Aside from wanting to be away from the sphere of his general rage and grumpiness, I really haven't known lately whether or not it would be better for me to go. Hence, this small "going," a test perhaps.

As I progress through this voyage, it comes to seem more and more as if both the physical and the mental hurts are shrieking to get out.

The ship is a great distraction.

We were on the Bridge for an hour and a half with the Captain this morning. He said it would take days to show us all the systems on the ship – and I'm sure he would enjoy doing it. His is a very lively intelligence, an engaging style and a contagious enthusiasm for his subject. Taking notes as fast as I could, I only got down a tenth of all he said. I wish I were better grounded in math and science!

41

He said that the ship is double-bottomed, that is, there are fuel and seawater ballast tanks between the cargo hold and the hull. Over the course of a passage, the use of fuel (800 tons between Panama and Tahiti, for example) will have a significant effect on the weight of the ship and thus how deeply she lies in the water (draft). So, obviously, will the weight of her cargo. An empty 40-foot container weighs 4.5 tons, a refrigerated container twice that. There are limits to how much weight they can carry. All this has to be taken into consideration when there are draft restrictions – 10.5 meters in Papeete, for instance. But weighing less, the ship is less stable in the water, which changes how the stacks of containers on deck affect how much the ship will list to the right or the left – a feedback loop. Containers have to be loaded carefully, the heaviest closer to or below the water line, the lightest higher up – for which there must be a constantly changing cargo plan available to every crane operator in every port. There can be six or seven containers per stack, and only the first three are fixed with steel tie-bars to the deck. Every container is fitted with four twist-locks, each lock capable of bearing up to 10 tons of lateral force, so that the upper tiers are also locked together. But the higher you go on a ship, the greater the radius of the roll – what the inclinometer measures at the hull is not what you experience eight stories up on the bridge, for example. It is not outside the realm of possibility that the wrong wave – given the wrong list of the ship in the water, given too much weight in the upper tiers of containers – could wash a container away or even endanger the ship.

To reduce the draft, you can't just pump out your ballast tanks. There are restrictions in some countries because of the possible introduction of invasive species in seawater transported from one part of the world to another. There is a problem in the Great Lakes, for example, with the zebra mussel that was introduced in ships' ballast and is wiping out native species. In other areas, particularly along coastlines where there is agrochemical run-off, a particular algae introduced in ballast has reproduced so quickly that it has robbed all the oxygen in the water and created marine deserts, "dead-zones" where nothing else can survive. The only place to discharge ballast "safely" is where there are 500 meters of ocean beneath your keel, so you can't pick up anything from the bottom and transport it where it might cause harm.

Right now, the ship is doing its deepest roll since I boarded in Panama. The Captain assures me that I haven't seen anything yet. He showed us on the compass that our course is one degree off due west (271). We have a beam swell from the south, and conditions will worsen as our voyage takes us closer and closer to the fierce winter storms racing one after another across the Southern Ocean. Between New Caledonia and Sydney, "we will really be making some music, and nothing as sedate as the salsa," he said. From Sydney to Melbourne it will be worse, to New Zealand even more so. "Then you'll really see what the seaman's life is like," he said looking at me. (Lila and Cristi are disembarking in Sydney.)

The Captain asked Third Mate to bring his sextant – a magnificent precision instrument – and let us each look through it to the horizon. "GPS will tell you where you are," he said, "but it won't tell you where to go in bad weather." The sextant "error" is only four miles; it will certainly get you where you want to go, just as its more primitive ancestors did hundreds of years ago (invented by the Chinese). In the northern hemisphere you will always know where north is from Polaris, the North Star. In the southern hemisphere there is no equivalent, but in either case taking a sextant reading from two stars, and knowing your exact time, is all you need to establish your position.

Lila asked him how far we can see with the naked eye from the Bridge of the ship. It depends on conditions, of course – clouds on the horizon, moisture in the air, reflections – on a day like today maybe 24 miles. What we see when the sun goes down, the Captain explained, isn't the real sunset. Because of the curvature of the earth and layers of vapor in the air, we are really seeing the *reflection* of the sunset.

The Captain showed us the gyro compass, the rudder indicator, the three-meter-long chart table with all the signal and country flags neatly cubby-holed above, the controls for the signal lights, vents and watertight doors, the fire alarm system, radar, automatic ship identification system, the central computer screen which displays longitude, latitude, speed, etc., the radios, the black box (just as on a plane, we were being recorded), and the all-important "telegraph" by which he directly controls the engine. And, of course the helm, a "steering wheel" that seemed much too small for the size and complexity of the ship. At that moment we were on autopilot, something we can use only in the open ocean, but Lila reached across the Captain and put both her hands on the wheel anyway. During any kind of maneuvers – in and out of ports, through the Canal – someone must stand there and steer the ship.

Of course, we were all curious about the cargo. The three-million dollar motor yacht taking up the equivalent of three 40-foot and five 20-foot times four tiers of containers on the foredeck, for all of which space the yacht's owner has paid, turns out not to be the most exotic bit of cargo

43

on board. There is a reefer filled with French champagne insured for a million euros, a Ferrari, perfumes, insulin, lobsters, explosives and a one-off 1952 Bentley with shark-skin seats belonging to some sheik. The value of the ship, the Captain said, is $45 million; the value of the cargo, $500 million. There's a complicated formula for calculating the fees to transit the Panama Canal but, as she is currently loaded, the *Louise* would pay about $50,000. Even so, the Captain assured us, ocean transport is still the cheapest way to go. To move a $400 chair across the Atlantic, for instance, would cost only about $12. He said our breakfast grapefruit probably traveled by sea from California to New York, and perhaps even to Savannah the same way; Canal transit and all, it costs less than truck or train, or certainly plane, to move something by ship from one part of the planet to another.

Day Seventeen, at Sea: Yesterday Lila revealed that there is a need for "gifts" in some ports. Where she heard this I don't know, but at lunch, after our informative tour of the Bridge and while the Captain was still sitting alone at the officers' table (when the others are there, the only language is Serbo-Croatian), Lila asked him directly if he gave liquor and cigarettes to the port authorities. I thought this was rather daring of her, but Lila sometimes charges ahead where angels fear to tread. The Captain made a distinction: sharing the ship's stores with the Pilots who are required to come on board in every port is just a courtesy among colleagues. In major ports in the developed world, "bribery is illegal." But in some ports, and he cited Limón on the Caribbean coast of Costa Rica, for example, gifts of whiskey and cigarettes to Customs and Immigration officials are the only way to get things done.

I had noticed that, after we left Tahiti, there was no more liquor on the Slop Chest list, and I was amazed that it had disappeared so quickly. Now I can guess where it went.

I woke to calmer seas this morning. During the night we passed through a storm with lightning and heavy rain lashing the portholes. Since Third Mate Denny had the kindness to pry loose the porthole screws with a long screwdriver so I could have some fresh air, I haven't been able to close the porthole as tightly, and in last night's rain it leaked. Manny gave me an old towel to absorb any moisture that comes in, and this morning I hung it up on a string to dry in the fresh breeze coming off our bow. Up on the observation deck, the wind was too strong for sunning, so I set up my little folding chair right outside the starboard E Deck door, where the noise from the engine is much louder. The exterior of E Deck wraps around the back of the superstructure to the port side, but I prefer to walk through the passage from one side to the other because on the outside route the engine roar through the E Deck vents is deafening.

I have been noticing that, with the shifts in the wind, some of the particulate matter from the stack is settling on the deck, little black bits that we scrape up with our shoes and carry around. Because of the ports she lands in, the *Louise* is in compliance with some of the strictest environmental regulations in the world, but I guess those rules don't extend to scrubbers or filters in the stacks.

It takes a while not to be alarmed by the smells on board. There are places where you can smell the heavy, oily fumes of diesel; whenever anyone is painting – a constant battle at sea against the ever recurring rust – the chemical smell of the anti-corrosive paint permeates the superstructure; and just outside my cabin, at the head of the stairwell, I get occasional puffs of bottled gas wafting up from the Galley just like smoke up a chimney. A freighter is a noisy, dirty, smelly beast. I wonder how they hide all this on passenger ships.

Lila knocked on my door at 6:30 this morning to tell me to hurry up to the Bridge to see the eclipse. What eclipse? Nobody had said anything about an eclipse. When I got up there, the First Mate let me look at the sun through the sextant – it was far too bright to look at with the naked eye, even that early in the morning, and even with a chunk eaten out of its side. He said the eclipse would have been total at around 5:00 a.m., but of course not visible where we were at the time. At breakfast, I asked Lila when she had heard about the eclipse, and she said that the Captain had mentioned it a few days before. I am under the impression that Lila likes knowing things we don't, and then springing them on us in a way that maximizes their dramatic impact. She also has our whole day planned in Lautoka, but I think I'm going to beg off – sounds too busy to me.

As in Tahiti, we'll come into port tomorrow at first light, a truly magical hour in these islands. Both Tahiti and Fiji are at a little less than 20 degrees latitude south of the Equator (Costa Rica is 10 degrees north), but both still well north of the Tropic of Capricorn. Looking at the big world map in the E Deck lounge, I see that the 40-degree south line runs right between the North and South Islands of New Zealand. With my finger, I traced the latitude lines north of the Equator. The forty-north line runs just south of Philadelphia. It can be very nasty in winter in Philadelphia. I'm hoping there are ocean currents to moderate the weather where I'm going, and I hope I have enough warm clothes!

There's an ancient romance to seafaring that still attracts people. Historically, going to sea represented danger, discovery and derring-do, the province of "real men," larger-than-life men, who knew how to endure incredible hardships and who had the experience and daring to make life and death decisions in an instant. When I remarked on the bridge again yesterday about how amazed I continue to be at those men who traveled the world's oceans with nothing but a sextant, Third Mate Denny reminded me that a lot of them had died – surely far more than ever lived to tell the tale. Conditions were harsh in the extreme. Simple survival was a challenge. This idea alone gets the adrenaline pumping in some people.

I suspect that the Captain is one of those people. Listening to his history, I imagine him to be some kind of male prodigy . . . or a prodigious producer of testosterone. Special Forces, sky diving, two tours in the French Foreign Legion (he was wounded), high-risk sports – parasailing, deep-sea diving, big game hunting (on the ground, not from a jeep), trophy fishing – whatever challenges him physically and mentally. He was given his first command of a ship at the age of 29. He has much to be proud of.

But I see a dangerous drift here. There's very little to distinguish the romance of seafaring from the machismo of the Foreign Legion, for instance . . . and from there to whatever attracts men to Special Forces in any military in the world . . . and from there to "professional soldiers," as the Captain calls them, mercenaries, and their world of he-men, of *übermenschen*. There, the challenge of survival means us versus them, kill or be killed, and utter contempt for anyone at the wrong end of your gun.

In the afternoon our course is more southwesterly, and we have the swell on our bow, along with a strong headwind. The containers on the foredeck are wiggling and groaning. We're seeing islands on both sides now, sandy atolls, so we're inside the reefs that almost encircle the Fiji Islands. Lautoka at dawn.

Passage Three
Fiji to New Caledonia
Without a *Centime*

Day Eighteen, Lautoka, Fiji: We pulled up in front of a giant sugar mill, behind a pile of what looked like chewed-up bagasse so enormous that the front-end loader scurrying around on top of it looked like a toy. The port of Lautoka was built by the British as a sugar port, and that's still what it is. Container traffic here is a relatively new addition, and it's a small cargo port even when compared to Papeete. Not as pretty either, the rocky headlands mostly bare, the only buildings in sight purely industrial.

A fat, black taxi driver in a Morris Mini with its steering wheel on the right and its springs sprung to the ground led us to believe he was the taxi called by the Port Agent to fetch us, and he asked in Indian/Fijian-accented English, "Where you want go, ladies?" Lila entered into the negotiations with a will, already suspecting him of trying to cheat us even before we settled into our seats. "Don't worry about the seatbelts," the driver said. (There weren't any.) A few kilometers down the King's Road, and after a flurry of mobile phone conversations, the driver pulled over and said we had to wait for the taxi that had *really* been called by the Port Agent. His stealing us had apparently raised quite a fuss. We sat there at the unshaded roadside for some minutes before Lila lost patience and suggested he call the offended taxi driver so that she could talk to him, which she did in no uncertain terms, and we were able to continue our journey – left only to imagine the consequences to any number of people of our escape.

Our guide, meanwhile, had taken no small offence at Lila's general pushiness, so we rode mostly in silence, although he did point out the "rock mountain." Lila asked him if there were volcanoes, and he said no, but it was obvious to us that the rock formations we were passing had been laid down by successive flows of lava. Aside from the mountains, the country was flat and covered with sugar cane, along with the rusted sheds and machinery needed to farm it. We saw no lovely beaches, just occasional stretches of turquoise water separating our island from the next.

Our objective was the Hindu Temple a little north of Nadi. I had read about this on line, and since I'll never get to India to see such things, this seemed like a good substitute. It's the largest such temple outside of India, in fact, and it was all made there and shipped to Fiji in pieces and reassembled to serve the large population of Indians who were brought to the island generations ago by the British to work the cane. There's a central building and several individual altars in the temple enclosure, and we had to approach the sacred ground on bare feet all the way from the graveled parking lot. The driver paid our entrance fee at a little booth off to the side, where they also sold paper plates with fruit offerings to the gods.

The effect overall was simply fantastic: no surface unelaborated with carvings, sacred images and paintings, the colors vibrant, even gaudy; the smoky odor of incense rising from numberless altars; a monotonic voice chanting ceaselessly into a public address system; shadowy interiors marked "For Devotees Only" with worshipers in saris, heads covered, carrying offerings of fruit or brilliant flowers to the altars, bowing low. We were able to photograph from outside, but not in.

From there our worthy driver took us downtown to a shopping district, where we picked up a few things in the pharmacy and the supermarket. I found a nice pair of seashell earrings to give to somebody, and looked for an international newspaper to no avail. A bottle of Absolut and a can of "Mexicana" peanuts imported from China ran me $70! Everything else was more reasonable. Lila double-checked the foreign exchange rate to make sure the taxi driver hadn't cheated us when he paid our entrance to the temple in Fijian dollars. "We need to show him we're on top of things," she said. I managed to say simply, "Lila, we're at his mercy; sit back and enjoy it."

We all wanted a massage, so the driver took us around the corner to the seediest little massage parlor any of us had ever seen. This was nothing like the luxury spa at least I had hoped for: a hard wooden bench in a tiny lobby, a cheaply printed yellow folder listing the offerings and prices, several girls idling about in uniforms waiting for something to do. Lila wanted a one-hour pedicure and foot massage; Cristi and I settled for a half-hour ($12) of back-pounding and pummeling on two side-by-side wooden tables with holes cut in them for our faces, and no place to put our things or our clothes except in a corner on the floor. It was obvious that this is where the poorer Indian ladies came for a bit of affordable luxuriating. As I stared through the hole in the table at the cheap vinyl in a green trellis pattern that had been pasted crookedly over the floor, I thought, "Later I'm going to be able to laugh at this." I am.

From the ridiculous to the sublime, we next went to the First Landing Resort, which our driver explained was the site where the first Fijians landed. "From where?" Lila wanted to know. "Oh, from the mainland," he answered and then quickly pointed out the national brewery we were passing and asked if we would like to stop at McDonalds for a soft drink – thus evading the next logical question: "Which mainland?"

The restaurant at First Landing is under cover and open to the sea, with palms and other familiar tropical plantings all around. The lunch was slow in coming (we tried the national beer, Vonu, not great), but the fish marinated in lime juice and coconut milk was superb. The place was not without its comedic aspect, however. Instead of a white-sand tropical beach (and Cristi assured us they do exist on the south coast), in front of the hotel was a man-made island in the shape of a giant footprint. First landing, footprint in the sand, get it? The site immediately lost all historical credibility for me.

On the way to the restrooms, I found the swimming pool, and asked the waitress if I could use it. We agreed that Lila and Cristi would go back to the Garden of the Sleeping Giant to see Raymond Burr's orchid collection and then swing by the hotel to pick me up on the way back to Lautoka. This was perfect. The day so far had been making me a little tense (in spite of the massage), and I was ready to do a bit of my own luxuriating in the water and then on a lounge chair in the sun. The water was chillier than I expected, but it felt good to move around without the earth's pull on my bones. There were few other people on the pool coping – a honeymoon couple, a well-oiled Aussie businessman talking loudly into his mobile phone. I had the place virtually to myself, surrounded by tropical vegetation, a noisy bird strutting mechanically around the chairs squawking insistently, just like the grackles at home, the afternoon sun bright in a perfectly clear sky.

By the time I had dressed, checked out the gift shop and made some notes about the day in the little travel diary given me by a friend, Lila and Cristi were back, and we tiredly pushed on toward the ship – I almost said "home," that's what it is to us now – bypassing what turned out to be our only opportunity to visit an Internet café.

I had remarked earlier to the Captain that I had never visited a country that was a military dictatorship before. He raised his eyebrows, but said nothing. Fiji is, but our taxi driver described it thus: "We have military government, good, no corruption." *A chacun à son goût.*

In spite of what a Fijian Immigration official had said to me in an email about my not requiring a visa to enter the country on my Costa Rican passport, the officials on the dock said I would. The same now applied to the Balkan officers, all of whom had entered Fiji in the past with no problems at all. Officialdom kept our passports all day while I was running around the island with Lila and Cristi. Nobody had even asked to see my ship's pass at the port security gate. The Captain shook his head. "Maybe they're afraid we would really want to live here," he said.

I have become accustomed to the poverty of taste in much of Costa Rica. In Fiji the unloveliness left over from British colonial rule is unavoidable, and the poverty is more severe. Perhaps the Captain summed up the experience of Fiji better than anyone. He told us that the first time he docked here as Master of a ship, the Port Agent showed up barefoot riding a bicycle. "I am not having Port Agent barefoot in my ship. No shoes, no coming in my ship. Out!"

We got away from Lautoka five or six hours early. The Captain said there was a big low pressure system behind us, and he hoped to outrun it. I woke up to feel the propeller engage around 1:30 in the morning, and once again I had that surge of thrill and wonder: *we're going to sea.*

Day Nineteen, at Sea: The wind churning up the sea and making F Deck uninhabitable is being generated by the low-pressure system to our northeast that is literally sucking all the air into it for hundreds of miles. The sea is busy, but the rolls, pitches and yaws aren't as long and deep as they were a few days ago. Bumpy would be a good word. I have long since abandoned trying to balance through the standing postures in my yoga routine – even in the relative "duck pond" around Fiji. Second Mate showed me on the chart that by noon tomorrow we'll be in the straits at the southern tip of New Caledonia, then in the port of Noumea on the west coast by 1600 hours or so (4:00 p.m.). The Captain had said that it'll be calmer with the whole of New Caledonia between us and the weather.

Another announcement came over the p.a. system at lunch today . . . another time zone to cross tonight! These jolts to one's biological clock – little hitches tripping us up as we cut an arc around the globe – are discombobulating. Even worse, our total inability to calculate how many hours we've lost or gained in all this progress across the Pacific (and for Lila and Cristi even farther) has become our mutual joke at lunch. Lila has a world SIM card in her mobile phone, so when we're in port she can call her sister or her son. My only way of keeping track of when it is where I've left is the little clock/calendar on the task bar of my computer screen; so today I reported to Lila that it was just 8:00 p.m. on the 13th in Washington, D.C., where she lives, two hours ahead of Costa Rica because of daylight saving time. But it's noon on the 14th where we are now. How many hours away is that? None of us can agree, so we just laugh and eat our soup.

Aside from the wind, the weather is sunny with only patches of cumulus zooming by, and the light on the sea is too dazzling to look at without sunglasses. I take a little break out on deck several times in the afternoon to warm up. The Captain refuses to accommodate our preference for higher temperatures in our cabins, saying that all the computer equipment on board needs to stay cool and dry. (Cristi said it got down to 17C in her cabin on the Atlantic crossing.) Opening my porthole helps to warm things up usually, but not when the wind is blowing on our bow as it is today. Add to the wind velocity the 20-knot speed of the ship, and a 15-mile-an-hour blow will feel like 35. They don't call it "wind-chill" for nothing.

Maybe I'm learning that pain doesn't have to make me panic. Aside from medicating myself into a stupor, which I don't want to do during the day, there's absolutely nothing I can do about it. At least on board, I can exercise, move around at will, and lie down when my neck starts to remind me I'm doing any one thing for too long. Days on shore can become downright unpleasant, but not wanting to dim the pleasure of my shipmates, I just separate myself and return to the ship if I can, or keep my mouth shut. This is why an all-day agenda, like the one Lila suggested we do yesterday, is so hard on me. It's not easy for me to be gracious when someone else is in charge – even unwittingly – of my comfort-level. So far, three weeks into it, this trip is proving to me two things: one, I can't really travel anymore and, two, I can survive it.

But I am also learning that there is a great psychological benefit to simply showing up. One has to appear at mealtimes – and every other time that has been prearranged – or people will worry. You don't want someone to come knocking on your door to ask what's the matter with you. When you're busy getting ready to show up, you are not feeling sorry for yourself.

And, as an eighty-year-old friend of mine says, "If you don't show up, nothing happens."

Day Twenty, at Sea: One advantage of the skipping time zones is that I'm usually awake in time to see the sunrise. The actual time varies daily as we move west-southwest, but when I turn the clock back when I'm ready for bed and note despairingly that it's not even eight o'clock, at least I have the consolation of an early rising. This morning I needed a sweatshirt, but I sat for 20 minutes on the top step and was rewarded with another magnificent show. Dark strips of cloud stretched across the eastern horizon, with barely a wash of pink where the sky met the sea. With little warning, the red blob of sun oozed forth from the primordial soup, then slowly back-lit the clouds above it, first in mauve, then rose, then gold, casting powerful rays both sky- and seaward, turning the water near the horizon into a bronze shield. Near the hull, the water was slate-gray, swelling softly under scattered clouds, an impenetrable element.

Land-ho! and Sail-ho! Just at ten o'clock, the shadowy bulk of New Caledonia penetrated the haze along the horizon to starboard and we saw a tall sloop with her jib bellied out cruising northward along the coast. This is the first boat of any kind we've seen on the open ocean since just before we docked in Tahiti. We've been moving in a perpetual bubble, miles and miles across; on the Bridge even the radar screen is blank. There's always activity around the ports, though, and we've seen some impressive yachts, although none so far under sail.

We still have a headwind, not as strong as yesterday's. The Captain explained that if we have winds out of the south, it'll be cold in New Caledonia; if out of the west, blowing from the land mass of Australia, it'll be warm. We're all praying for warm! This will be my last opportunity to get in the water for a month, the temperatures in Sydney being plenty cold (the Captain reported 9C there during my first week on board).

Seen from the northeast, the New Caledonian coast was mountainous and tree-covered and forbidding. There appeared to be no development at all on the windward side. Once we were in the narrow straits, the land fell abruptly in high precipitous cliffs, the waves crashing on the rocks below. Very quickly a crisp black and white pilot boat pulled alongside and two men clambered aboard using the rope and block ladder we had thrown over the side – not a leap for the faint of heart. As we rounded the southern point and turned the corner onto the leeward shore inside the barrier reef, the sea went as calm as a lake and the ship suddenly stopped rolling. The water near the hull turned a translucent teal, graduating to pure turquoise along the white-sand beaches. To our left, the relatively narrow bit of ocean that separates New Caledonia from Australia. Out on the sunny deck, it feels warm – I'm in luck.

It took another three hours before we wound our way into Noumea harbor, a long sinuous channel well-protected from any weather. Because another ship was still in our berth, we had to drop anchor and wait. Second Mate had pegged our arrival for 1600 hours. With a tug pushing our stern and our bow thruster churning up the sand under our hull, we nudged up against the fenders on the dock at exactly 4:07. How in the world can they predict the arrival of a behemoth like the *Louise* with such accuracy?

Over time we learn to recognize the different sounds of the ship, which sometimes seem no more than a throbbing inside my own chest. After so long on a straight line between ports, we hear/feel the rudder when it starts to turn the bulk of the ship into a new course. When we're coming into harbor, these turns are very pronounced, and the whole ship shudders with the force required to move that massive blade. Through the many course changes needed to get her alongside the dock at Noumea, it felt as if the *Louise* were groaning.

I was shocked at lunch when Lila told us she had made herself some toast in the Galley at ten in the morning. She had missed breakfast, was hungry, and saw no reason why she shouldn't go into the pantry between the Mess and the Galley – Manny's private preserve – and pop a piece of bread into the toaster. Looking around for the plate of cheese that's usually on our table, she dared to open the pantry refrigerator. Coming in and finding her *in flagrante delicto,* Manny had been visibly upset. I could imagine so. But then she went on to tell us she had told him, "Don't worry, Manny, I know how to make my own toast!"

On a stool in the Officers' Lounge later in the day, with the Chief Engineer and the Captain, Lila repeated her story with just a hint of braggadocio. I looked at Karlo behind the bar. Karlo looked over at the Captain.

The Captain fixed Lila in his gaze and kept his tone dead-even. "Do you have a sanitary book?"

"What's a sanitary book?" Lila asked.

"Nobody goes into Galley that doesn't have a sanitary book. Inspectors come on board, they find somebody in the Galley who isn't supposed to be there, they make big problem for Captain, ship, Company, everybody. Nobody on this ship is going into Galley except Cook and Messman that have sanitary book."

Karlo relieved the tension a bit with a story about how the engineering crew of one ship he served in had had to make repairs to a dumbwaiter between the Galley and the Officers' Mess, and his then-captain caught them in the Galley with all their grease and tools and kicked them out in a rage.

I'm sorry to admit I felt a small stab of pleasure that Lila was visibly under the Captain's disapproval. Sometimes she treads a little further than the bounds of respect.

Last night I learned from the Chief Engineer that they had replaced a piston in the main engine the day before. *A piston.* One of those five-meter-high jobs hanging aft of the engine. This little chore took five men working nonstop from 3:00 a.m. to 10:00 that night, and we only briefly saw Karlo in his overall covered with grease from head to foot when he dashed into the Mess during dinner with something for the Captain to sign. When he told me all this yesterday evening, I asked of the piston, "Can you fix it?" He scoffed, "Yeah, we can fix anything." I'm impressed.

Average engine life these days is 36,000 hours, and the *Louise*'s engine has logged more than that.

Day Twenty-one, Noumea, New Caledonia: We had been warned that it's very hard to pay for anything in Noumea without local currency, but we never imagined it would be impossible to get local currency. Lila had luck at an ATM machine, but I tried two change machines, two ATMs, and two banks with no luck at all. Fortunately, before we went our separate ways, Lila once again came through with a loan of 2,500 francs, presumably enough to buy me some time in an Internet café and pay my taxi fare back to the ship. I had brought my computer along in hopes of connecting directly and being able to use Outlook, but the young woman at the café looked at me as if I were from Mars, gave me an English keyboard and sat me down in front of one of their computers. After an hour or so catching up on mail and sending off my scribblings to at least some people (I tried several ways to copy the distribution list into a gmail, but no go), I hauled my computer outside again in search of an English-language newspaper (no luck there either) and more opportunities to be refused cash. The last time I traveled, which I have to admit was in 2003, any bank would advance me cash on my international Visa card. Not in Noumea. And I couldn't exchange cash dollars either unless I had an account at the bank. After the Internet café, I wasn't even sure I had enough for taxi fare. Nothing makes one feel so lost in a foreign city as being without the means of escape!

By this time I was desperate for a bathroom, and I found a pretty little sidewalk café at one corner of the park. *"Où sont les toilettes?"* got me a key to a clean restroom even without my ordering anything, so of course I felt obliged to stay for lunch, as long as they took credit cards. It was pleasant there at my little table, even without the best view of the pond in front of the café and all the beautiful plantings in the park. Noumea is a bright, clean city with a wonderful series of *places* running through the middle of it, although the French seem always to be French, no matter where they are. I've always experienced them as a little chilly and impatient, and that was true in Noumea as well. And both here and in Tahiti, I had the powerful impression that there are only two classes of people in these colonies still ruled from Paris: the French and the Not-French, which means the Polynesians (and the occasional hapless tourist). The French ate and drank with their usual self-assurance, while the Not-French waited table. With just a slight shift in the vegetation around me, I could have been in Paris itself. The food, of course, was excellent.

I felt much fortified after my lunch, so I gathered up my computer and went in search of the taxi-stand that our morning taxi driver had mentioned was nearby. Went around one whole *place* in the midday sun and saw nothing. Once again I had to ask several people on the street in my limited French (suddenly I am a quailing idiot!), and even though they all pointed in the same general direction, I saw nothing obvious until a little green-and-white taxi pulled up in front of what looked like a bus stop just caddy-corner from my café. No sign for the unwary tourist, but I waited there and one came along pretty quickly. Fortunately my borrowed funds held.

The taxi could go no farther than the port security gate, of course, and this meant another 15-minute walk lugging that damn computer through hundreds of stacks of containers. From the gate I could see the Bridge of the *Louise*, so I had a general idea of where I was going, which was a good thing because, once among the stacks it wouldn't be hard to get lost. At every corner I looked not only to the right and left, but above. The vehicles for moving those boxes around are bizarre enough to be in a science-fiction movie, capable of picking up containers with their huge pincers from on top, below and sideways, and they move with alarming speed. I finally emerged from an alley near the two huge dock cranes that were working away alongside our ship, the containers careening weirdly overhead at the rate of one every two minutes. There were lots of stevedores standing around in hard-hats, and not one of them said, "Careful, lady!" I just waited for a lull between crane-loads and dashed for the accommodation ladder. One of our deckhands waved and came part-way down to relieve me of my computer, which at that point felt as if it weighed 30 pounds. I was grateful to be back on board!

Until I remembered that the elevator was out. Its certificate had expired on July 5th, so it has been kept out of operation whenever we're in port, just in case a nosey inspector should come on board. This meant that, from the dock, I had to walk up over seven flights of stairs (the accommodation ladder is one and a half) to get to my cabin. Once on E Deck, I made myself a cup of tea in the lounge and put up my feet. If I ever do this again, I'll follow Cristi and Lila's example and get a backpack and carry a much smaller computer!

It was a relief finally to hear from Roger – three emails, including a confirmation copy of the one he had sent to the Captain's address that never reached me. Just as we were in Tahiti, he had written again, to my gmail address, but the timing of my Internet access was such that I missed his letter. Finally, in Noumea there was a nice detailed note from home, and I found myself beginning to feel a little homesick.

Now, don't I feel silly for all my doubts? No, I remind myself. Everything I said is still true, even if I'm relieved to know he's all right and that everything there is fine; even though I appreciate how much it took for him to two-finger type that nice letter; even though he was probably sincere when he said he missed me. He mentioned the rain, the dogs, our houseguests, our continuing financial uncertainty. Nothing has changed. If my being away so long does anything to remind both of us not to take each other for granted, at least for a while, that will be something. But now it's more than ever clear to me that, if we want to go on living together, we must drastically improve the quality (and quantity) of our communications with each other. And that will mean establishing some new level of trust.

Is this doable? I don't know. But I find myself arriving at new insights in this slow progress across the Pacific. Roger is a very private, even secretive, person. I'm guessing that, when he was a child this secretiveness was the only territory he could carve out for himself that was safe from his mother. I, on the other hand, used my head as a battering ram against the brick wall of my father's indifference. In marrying, we have chosen well, we have chosen what we know. But I still haven't a clue, after all these years of living together, how to take the first step that will open this door for both of us.

Watching the loading in the afternoon, warming myself on deck on the starboard side, I saw yet another variation on cargo-loading that I hadn't seen before. The 20-foot containers have two slots in their decks spaced perfectly apart for a super-duper fork-lift. This beast slides its tines into the slots, juggles the box aloft and carries it over to a steel form on the dock that just exactly holds two 20-footers end-to-end. From above, the massive crane lowers a corresponding frame with five paddle-shaped "feelers" that guide it precisely onto the tops of the two containers. It then locks into four of their corner locks and picks up both of them at the same time, swinging them up and over into their pre-arranged position on deck. While they're being lowered to the deck (or onto a stack of containers on the deck), the fork lift quickly maneuvers two other containers onto the form and jockeys them into position just in time for the crane to come gobble them up. It's wonderful to imagine the mind that dreamed up this whole system. Did he play video games?

Passing the door of the lounge last evening, the Captain greeted me on his way to an early supper, saying we'd be moving in ten or 15 minutes. I went out on deck to watch, as two of the crew were packing up the accommodation ladder. This alone was a complicated piece of business, as it collapses after the sustaining cables are removed and is then winched up to the level of the rail and turned over on its side out of the way. I waited, as the sun went down and the deck lights came on. No one was left on the dock. "Who is going to cast us off?" I wondered. Then, way off our bow, a tiny white van came zipping up to the ship and one man hopped out near our bow line. It then dropped off a second man at the first spring line, a third at the next, and finally two men at the stern line way around the dock on the beach. One by one, our giant winches engaged to pull us a little closer to the dock, thus easing the tension on the hawsers enough to give each of them some slack; one by one, each little man (from my perspective!) unhooked the heavy line from its bollard and dropped it into the sea. When only one line was left, the ship's propeller ground into motion, and I could see the dark waters churning between the hull and the dock. Slowly, slowly our stern began to pull away, and I raced across the ship to the port side to see a brightly-lit tugboat connected to us by about 50 meters of towline. Each time the tug gained a purchase in the water, the towline snapped taut, hurling millions of gemlike droplets into the dark.

We were away from the dock at 6:00 p.m. Manny came out on deck to watch the last 10 minutes or so with me, and I realized that, as lowly and humble as his position in the ship is, he too has a fascination for ships and the sea. He went in to serve dinner, and I looked up into the luminescent sky to see a perfect quarter-moon, with the Evening Star riding her coattails, almost at the meridian.

Taking my fresh air after dinner up on port-side E Deck, only a dim glow in the western sky (the direction we were heading), the shore lights gleaming on the near horizon, suddenly I saw some flashing lights moving quickly up on our stern, and I realized it was the pilot boat, come to pick up her men. We seemed to be steaming full ahead – at least it felt that way with the breeze on our nose – and the pilot boat was making time to catch up with us. She approached our bow wave, churning up a considerable one of her own, and I watched as she slowly matched her speed to ours. You can't see the bow from E Deck, but I leaned over the rail and saw the pilot boat dip in toward our bow once, then a second time – during which incredibly brief moments both men leaped aboard – and she peeled off to our port, one-by-one dimming her deck lights, and, with just her red and green running lights on the mast, her wake still foaming white behind her, she was gone.

Later the captain told us that the pilots had to get off early, while the ship was still inside the barrier reef, because the waves outside were too high to allow for a leaping disembarkation! He showed us on the chart the tiny channel we had had to negotiate on our own, without benefit of local piloting. Fifteen meters either way, and we would have been on the rocks. He also said that more than once he has had to put in to an unscheduled port on the wrong side of English Channel to drop off his Rotterdam pilot because the North Sea was too rough to land him.

I'm feeling more comfortable with Manny now that we've had that shared moment of departure from the Noumea dock. Perhaps living for 20 years in a culture I'm not native to has made me super-sensitive to the social nuances as well as to the dangers of behaving in ways that seem normal but can be big-time gaffes in another country. I had a question about how, and how much, to tip Manny, so in my first week on board I asked both Lila and Cristi – separately – what they intended to do. Cristi said she would "do something" for Manny before she disembarked. Lila was even vaguer. In my researches about sea-voyaging I had read that it was customary to tip both the Steward and the Messman every week, but I had been hoping to get clearer guidelines as to the amount (especially considering that Manny fills both functions). Lila even brought this up with the Captain when we were asking him about what we should give the crew, and he said that whatever we arranged with Manny was between us and Manny. No help there. I was left to consult my own heart and wallet.

After seven days on board, I stayed in my cabin while Manny changed the sheets and tidied up. We hadn't spoken much at that point because he was shy about his English and I could barely understand his few heavily accented, whispered remarks, but that day I wanted to introduce the subject of the tip.

"Do you ever get to go ashore, Manny?" I asked.

He smiled faintly. "Sometimes, ma'am."

"Good, then I would like to give you something so you have a little extra to spend when you do," I said and handed him a discretely folded bill.

He demurred, embarrassed to accept. "Oh, that's not necessary, ma'am."

I kept my hand extended. "I know it's not, Manny, but it gives me pleasure to give it to you." And he reluctantly took it and slipped it into his pocket.

The next week I expected to be in the gym when Manny came to change the linens, so I left the bill on my pillow, the way I would do for a hotel maid. When I got back, Manny had carefully left it in plain view on the bedside table. Frustrated, I stuffed it in my pocket, determined to give it to him at lunch. For this I managed to be the first person in the Mess, and when I handed it to him, he seemed even more embarrassed, as if he were afraid someone else would see us.

For several days after, I worried that offering him money might be offensive to him, but I had no way of investigating the Filipino culture to help me out in what was potentially a delicate situation. I was afraid he would see me as a pushy, insensitive *gringa*. All I could do was go with what I *felt* to be correct. The man worked seven days a week, cleaning all the cabins and serving all the meals and he did it with good will. He deserved my appreciation. Finally, at the end of my third week, I remained in my room so as to give him his tip in person and privately, and by now – whether I was being culturally brutish or not – he seemed to have gotten used to the idea that this was going to be a weekly event and he was a little less embarrassed to go through with it. What a relief!

Passage Four
New Caledonia to Australia
Turning the Corner at the Opera House

Day Twenty-two, at Sea: Two points describe a line, three points a curve. After New Caledonia, our third port, I suddenly feel a sense of having crossed a lot of geography. It *is* a lot, in fact. During the "continuation of our bridge tour" this morning, as we poured over the charts, the Captain said that, by the time we get to Sydney, we will have crossed approximately 7,800 nautical miles from Panama – more than a third of the way around the globe.

The *Louise* is back to her old pitching ways, plowing a furrow through the Pacific at 19.6 knots over ground. Her bearing is 240, still west-southwest, the 15-knot wind just on her port quarter, heading 220, which means we're taking the wind almost on the bow and the ship isn't yawing much, just bouncing into the troughs and back. Looking at how far the bow was rising and falling in relation to the horizon, the Captain said the difference between the top and bottom of her trajectory – the bow amplitude, he called it – was about nine meters. We were all standing around on the bridge weaving slightly back and forth, and flexing our calves, ankles and toes in what has now become an automatic response to the shifting deck – sea legs!

I have always loved looking at charts. The Captain showed us a detail of the straits at the south end of New Caledonia and the features of the harbor at Botany Bay, where we'll dock south of Sydney. He pointed out that we had been berthed in Noumea in only 12.4 meters of water when our draft had been 9.9. Not a lot of wiggle room. He asked Third Mate to pull down the "alphabet" – over a 1,000 symbols one has to recognize in order to read a chart. Using this, we could see the lines of the prevailing currents at different seasons of the year, and there were even long arcs indicating how many degrees off true magnetic north one is at any given position on the planet. (The North Pole is not magnetic north, although it is called "true north," the Captain reminded us. The *Louise*'s compasses are set for magnetic north, and at that moment we could see the difference where we are in the Pacific to be about 13 degrees.) With his finger, he traced our projected route, drawn in pencil from New Caledonia to Botany Bay, pretty straight shooting except for two small course corrections taking us in stages from a bearing of 240 to 218, nothing to move out of the way for until we are in the approaches to the harbor, where he hopes to have us by 3:00 a.m. on the 19th. He's making speed because he wants to beat out two other ships in line for the dock. Botany Bay is a very busy port, but small, and ships often have to wait their turn. With luck we'll be alongside by six in the morning.

I asked the Captain to explain how the Automatic Identification System works. It's a VHF (very high frequency) radio signal sent by all ships at sea that includes the name of the vessel, size, draft, last port of call, next port, type of cargo, bearing, and number of people on board, in addition to more technical information. If the Captain sees a vessel on the radar, he clicks on the AIS to get the details, and this way he'll know in what direction she will pass the *Louise* – forward, astern, port or starboard. I asked him about pirates. "They turn it off," he said, in a tone to suggest I had asked a stupid question.

Next he asked Third Mate to pull the emergency equipment out of a cupboard on the port side of the bridge. There was a rocket-powered life line for shooting out to someone in the water. He said it was powerful enough to blow a hole in the bulkhead. There was a rocket-launched parachute that reaches an altitude of 500 meters, colored bright red – the distress color at sea – as well as flares that can be seen miles away. There was a radar transponder, in case the ship goes down, that will send her position to a marine coordinating center that will alert any vessels in the area to come to her aid (airplanes have similar equipment on board). He took us out on the starboard wing to see the "smoker" attached to the lifebuoy. Throwing the lifebuoy into the water after a man overboard will automatically engage the smoker, so it will be easy to locate the victim later. Ships of this size aren't very maneuverable – it would take a long time for the *Louise* to slow and turn around to come back in aid of someone in the water. Of course, we were impressed by all of these toys . . . except they're dead-serious pieces of equipment that every sailor must know how to use. The more we learn about the workings of the ship, the more we appreciate the training seamen have to have.

We got a sample of hands-on training when the fire alarm went off at 3:30 in the afternoon. We had had advance warning of this – and Cristi had already described the drill she experienced in the Atlantic – but of course I was engrossed in what I was doing when that ear-splitting alarm went off just when they said it would, and I had to bustle about and get into my shoes, grab the bulky immersion suit bag and high-tail it up two flights of stairs to the bridge, which is our station in any emergency. Lila and Cristi were way ahead of me. "You won!" I gasped. From then on we watched and listened as the Captain communicated by walkie-talkie with all emergency stations while the other officers and crew simulated a fire in the engine room. There are very specific procedures to follow, and they talked everything through, including the spread of the fire to the cargo hold. Finally the Captain sounded the "Abandon Ship" alarm and we all went trooping down to the port boat deck (Lila stayed above) where Cristi and I watched as, one by one, the men climbed into the life boat and started the engine, something all of them must be able to do. Even Manny was there in his hardhat and boots, and First Mate put us passengers in his charge during any emergency.

As we watched the drill, Second Mate Enrique regaled us with his experiences in a chute-launcher. We had seen several of these on tankers in the Canal. The bright orange, fully enclosed life boat is perched on a chute aft of the super structure and when it's launched it is shot nose-first from a height of several stories into the water well clear of the stern. Second Mate told us you shouldn't do a chute-launch if you have cardiac problems. (Was he suggesting that people at risk of heart attack go down with the ship?). "That really separates the men from the girls," he said. "Well!" I shot back, "I'm just a girl and I don't pretend to be anything else!" Enrique laughed. Fortunately, our life boat is suspended from davits, part of a launching apparatus, and parallel to the deck, just as we've all seen in the movies. Enrique explained that if we're strapped correctly inside the boat, it will right itself in the water so that the portholes and hatches are facing up. Comforting. Each boat can take 32, there are two boats, and we passengers are assigned to the starboard boat. "But the best lifeboat," Enrique said, "is the ship." That's not the first time we've had an officer stress the importance of safety on board.

Next the Captain wanted to run us through an emergency steering drill. If there's a fire in the engine room, the generators are immediately shut down and there's only a backup power supply – batteries, in the case of lights, backup generator for the rudder, which has to be wired into the main circuit board controlling the steering pumps. All of us scurried from the boat deck down the ladders to Main, and from there to the roaring stern and down a hatch into the steering room, where Cristi and I plugged our fingers in our ears so as not to go prematurely deaf while the Chief Engineer explained in detail how to connect the alternate power supply. If anybody heard a word of his dissertation over the noise of the engines and the propeller, I'd be surprised; it was agony standing there. Finally, I could read the Chief's lips say, "Any questions?" to which nobody said a thing, and we were all released. I dashed back up to the Main Deck and hurried along the port side to the ladder, noting that the bow wave had gotten a lot bigger while I wasn't looking. We were obviously heading more into the wind, and it was cold on deck.

Later when I talked to Karlo in the lounge, I remarked that an emergency lighting system was certainly a comforting idea, because in the dark people are much more apt to panic. He said there would be no backup lighting in the engine room – in case of fire there, everything gets shut down. "How do you see?" I asked. "You have the light of the fire," he said!

In the evening, we were entertained with container stories – our officers have seen just about everything. Containers are sealed, bonded cargo and only in U.S. and European ports are they weighed before they are loaded on the ship. Sometimes in other ports the cranes themselves incorporate scales – but in those cases the weighing is not official, it's only for the protection of the crane itself. It is typical, the Captain said, for meat shippers in non-U.S. and European ports to declare a lesser cargo weight than is the real number – 25 tons of frozen lamb chops, for example, instead of 30. If they can get away with it, the extra five tons ride free. But during loading, the Captain keeps an eye on the ship's draft. Too many such little lies and the ship will lie lower in the water than she's supposed to. He has been known to insist that a container be taken off his ship. "The draft doesn't lie," he said.

He also told us that it would be easier to ship a container-full of cocaine than to try to hide it somewhere on the hull below the water line. In Colombian, Central American and Jamaican ports, U.S. taxpayers pay for underwater inspectors – complete with wet suits, oxygen tanks and masks – to paddle along ships' hulls looking for illicit goods. Meanwhile, unmanned subs full of drugs are traveling freely along the Pacific coast between Colombia and Mexico. There isn't enough money in the world to stop this traffic.

Not only can you feel the rudder move, you can feel the change in the way the ship strides through the sea. Suddenly the *Louise* is hitting the water differently, almost as if the sea were a solid thing. On our first course change out of Noumea, as we turned just a few points closer to the wind, the bow slapped into the ocean with a real jerk. At sunset the water is the color of steel. Twenty-one hours away from Sydney, at this more southerly latitude it even *looks* colder.

Day Twenty-three, at sea: This is Lila and Cristi's last full day on board, and Cristi spent the day calmly sitting on deck watching for the Australian coastline, which she finally spotted around four o'clock, while Lila was in a tizzy of repacking her four suitcases – she came prepared to spend almost two years abroad. But finally, the three "ladies" were able to sit quietly out on starboard E Deck enjoying what will probably be the last opportunity for sunning (albeit in long pants and jackets) for several weeks. We were huddled in the lee, but the sun was only a pale cousin of what it had been in the tropics, and when it hid behind a cloud the temperature dropped quickly.

We had agreed on a three-kilo tin of chocolates as a thank-you gift to the officers and crew. We deliberated on the wording of the note, and Cristi came up with some medical tape to affix it to the gift. In the morning I dropped this off in the Crew's Lounge on my way to the gym, realizing full-well that the Balkan officers would not share in the bounty, even though we tried to make it clear that the gift was for everyone. If we had left it in the Officers' Lounge, the crew (and the other officers) never would have seen it. We had to settle for the greatest good for the greatest number.

At lunch there was a lot of conversation about how to get into Sydney and whether or not I would go with Lila and Cristi. There's a Seaman's Mission bus that stops at the port security gate every half-hour that will take us to their non-denominational mission downtown. From there my shipmates will be trying to find a reasonable hotel, and I will taxi on to the Opera House, the one thing in Sydney I really want to see. Lila was getting anxious about all this, and preferred that I go alone, fearing that depending on their arrangements might slow me down and I wouldn't get to do everything I'd hoped. Cristi had the kindness to sell me $100 Australian dollars – nothing I would ever have been able to find in Costa Rica.

In the evening the Captain brought a CD into the lounge on which he'd copied some photos for me to take home. I ran upstairs for my laptop and we all watched in utter amazement scenes of the bow that he had taken from the Bridge during a North Atlantic storm – the waves breaking *over* the containers. I accused him of trying to scare me, since he insists the weather is going to be *bad* as we move further south. Then he opened the second photo file on the disc and almost dropped us on the floor with a series of pictures of container ships that – through storm, bad luck or sheer stupidity – had all or partly lost or damaged their cargo. There was a photo of a container accidentally dropped by a crane operator onto the cab of a truck; a ship's bow that had rammed the dock at speed; another loaded ship with its bow sunk on the bottom at the side of the dock, containers and all; and a short video of a crane breaking up in the attempt to lift a container that was too heavy for it – the operator and several people were killed in that one. I could imagine the insurance adjusters had nightmares over some of these accidents. But the Captain's message to us was, it's a dangerous business and you've got to really know what you're doing. He knocked on wood: "I haven't lost a container yet."

He's got an ulcer, though.

Day Twenty-four, Becalmed: Or the modern-day equivalent. We were steaming proudly ahead all day yesterday in hopes of getting a priority berthing at Botany Bay, but no such luck. After midnight, the engines shut down, and now, along with three other vessels I've counted so far, we're out here drifting in the current, where it's too deep to anchor, awaiting the pleasure of the Pilot Station – which now seems to be unlikely before 4:00 p.m. today. Lila and Cristi will still be able to disembark, but I will probably miss the Opera House. Once we're docked, loading operations will continue through the night so the ship can get away early in the morning. We were due to be here for only 15 hours. That's worst-case, but I must be prepared for it. Maybe there'll be compensation in the form of wi-fi in the port? Everything in my computer needs updating.

Now Lila comes with the news that, even if the pilot is on board by 4:00, it'll be 6:30 before we'll be able to disembark (immigration, etc.), and we need to figure an hour to get into town, so what would I be able to see? What would be open? She tells me that from the Bridge there may be a possibility of spotting the Opera House through the binoculars around 9:30, but it turns out she misheard the Captain. We would have to be closer to shore, looking directly down the long funnel of Sydney Harbour. Still,

I was able to see part of the Harbour Bridge and the towers of the city and the high chalky cliffs to the north. The reddish pall over Sydney is sand windblown from the desert.

The Pilot Station calls while I'm on the Bridge, putting back our time to 4:30. The Captain says we'll certainly load all night, maybe get away as early as dawn if we have three gantries available. He won't know until he sees the Port Agent. Now the engines are engaged at dead-slow to reposition the *Louise* in the current. This will happen a number of times before we're finally able to head in. I'm disappointed but remind myself that the destinations are really the least important part of this journey. And maybe I can set my foot on Australian soil in Melbourne.

The day is clouding over. The sea is the color of sheet-metal. We wait.

Four-thirty in the afternoon, and we continue to drift here, east-southeast of Sydney, the city clearly visible on the horizon, a great gray cloud piled up behind it. What wind there is seems to be coming from that direction, so we may have weather. I haven't been up on the Bridge since early afternoon, when Second Mate Enrique told me that the pilot has now been postponed till 6:30. He opined that, since we're scheduled to fuel in Botany Bay, and we can only do that in daylight, it's probable that we'll be in port all morning, which will give me a chance to go ashore. I had just been searching for Cristi to sell back the Australian dollars she had sold me, when my hope was thus renewed.

This is the first experience we have had of just . . . waiting. The Captain constantly emphasizes the unpredictability of being at sea, but so far the schedule has been met within minutes. We even gained a few hours when we were running before the weather, but those hours are now long gone. Second Mate told me that on one voyage the Company had ordered the ship off to Melbourne first, which has to cost a bundle of money. Since we're scheduled for fuel – which takes many hours to pump on board – Enrique thinks a diversion south unlikely. I hope so. I have been looking forward to a couple of days by myself before the new passengers come on board at Melbourne.

Just before dinner, the Captain came into the lounge to announce to Lila that all is arranged: on the dock at 6:30, at the port gate by 8:00, the Seaman's Mission bus at 8:30. She had just been speculating on the need to stay on board an extra night (but having paid for three nights over what turned out to be the final schedule, she feels she'll be getting at least a little of her money back).

Then, at 7:00, when the *Louise* was still dawdling out here in the current, Third Mate came to tell Cristi and Lila that they would indeed be spending the night on board, and that he was terribly sorry but the pilot was late and everything was pushed back a few hours. They were relieved that they would not be hustling Lila's four suitcases around the port in the dark and trying to find accommodation that late in the day. Lila had called her sister in Switzerland to ask her to get on line to see if there were any hotel rooms available, and she had come up with a "boutique hotel" at $125 a night, but Lila didn't want to book until she knew if the Seaman's Mission could come up with something downtown a little more "reasonable." A lot of flurry.

The nighttime approach to Sydney was worth all the waiting and trouble, however. We wrapped ourselves up warmly and stood out on deck watching the city lights as we progressed slowly north along the shore and then cut a wide arc before describing a direct line for the entrance to the port. The tower in the city center seemed to be suspended above a perfect cloudbank of lights, like a beacon from heaven. We could see the runway lights of the airport and just to the right the lights on the gantries of the port. We picked up a tug near the entrance, and watched as she pushed at our stern to line us up with our berth. Then the enormous propeller of the *Louise* shifted into reverse, sending a jolt through the whole ship, and the black water at our stern churned violently as we were nudged gently, aft end first, into the dock. The lines and winches did the rest, the linesmen on shore wearing hardhats and reflective vests (unlike in the islands, where the safety measures were a lot more casual). The lights of the port, all around us and on the other ships in the harbor, were dazzling. It was beautiful, but I couldn't help wondering at the cost of all the power required to perform the dazzle.

Day Twenty-five, Sydney: It started out to be a disappointing morning. A little before 8:00, I learned that shore leave would expire at 11:00, and that there should be a Seaman's Mission bus at the port gate at 8:45. My shipmates would have to wait on board for Customs officials to check their luggage, so they decided they would call a taxi from the gate. We said our third set of goodbyes, and off I dashed, signing out and trundling down the accommodation ladder to wait for a shuttle bus.

One of the things I forgot to bring with me is a watch. With Lila and Cristi, both of whom wear watches, I was never without the time. But, in the bus shack by the security gate, there was no way to know, and I began to feel the time was dragging past the bus's scheduled stop. As I sat in the converted 20-foot container on a vinyl chair, huddled against the cold, pummeled by the sound of the trucks grinding their gears as they went through the gate, I began to feel very discouraged and doubtful that I would see any more of Australia than the straggly pine trees and tank farm across the road. My one dream had been to see the Sydney Opera House. And now it looked as if I would never have time – even if I asked the guard to call me a taxi – to get into town and back for the ship's sailing.

Then Cristi and Lila showed up, and I waited until the guard passed them and all Lila's luggage through the gate. By then it was 9:15 – I had waited over an hour – and I decided to abandon my little quest and return to the ship. The shuttle driver said, "That was quick," when I re-boarded, and I explained what had happened. He was sympathetic and suggested maybe a water taxi could get me there. He wasn't sure about how long it would take, and he said, "So what if it costs a couple hundred dollars? This is your only chance."

I thought about it briefly, and then decided the time was probably too short even to try to organize something like that. Getting off the bus, I thanked him, but by then I was feeling close to tears. The feeling got closer as I climbed the accommodation ladder and all the way up to my cabin, but I decided not to let myself be overwhelmed by self-pity, and I gathered up my dirty clothes and went down the passageway to the laundry. I could hear the Captain and someone else talking in the lounge as I walked by, but I didn't look in.

Two minutes later I was back in my cabin and Third Mate Denny was at my door telling me the Captain wanted to speak to me. When I entered the lounge, the Captain grinned broadly and said, "This is lady from Seaman's Mission." We shook hands, and the Captain explained that shore leave had been extended to four o'clock, and Sister Mary of the Mission was going to drive me to the Opera House. Only an hour and a half later, after much waiting and milling around and finally seated in the Mission's little white van with the Captain, the Chief Engineer, the Bosun and the Second Engineer, all of us oohing and ahing over the beautiful city of Sydney as we rolled by, did it occur to me to be amazed that all these people wanted to see the Opera House too, and that it was their combined idea – when the sailing hour was delayed – to take me there together. The Beach

Boys were singing "California Girls" on the radio, and I had one of those incredible experiences of disconnect from my old life, mixed with pure joy and gratitude to these foreign seamen, fellow voyagers, who were total strangers to me less than a month ago.

It was a spectacular day. The weather was chilly, but the sky was brilliantly blue and clear. From the back of the van, I could see little in front of us, so that when we rounded a stone embankment and the Opera House suddenly rose up on our left like a giant bird flashing its brilliant white wings, I involuntarily gasped, grabbed my camera, tumbled out onto the pavement and started walking toward it in awe.

It is rare, among the works of man, to find something so absolutely perfect that it is almost godly.

No photograph can prepare you for the overwhelming sight of the Sydney Opera House right on top of you. We walked around it, taking pictures from all angles and taking pictures of each other with the Opera House in the background. The joy seemed contagious. Then we started walking, walking, walking, all around Circular Quay and the ferry docks to the side of the harbor nearer the Harbour Bridge and an area called The Rocks, where the first British prisoners were landed to settle here or die. The Chief Engineer was on a mission to find the monument he had seen in 1988, when he was working in a bulk cargo ship that was parked here for a couple of weeks during the national bicentennial, when all the tall ships of the world had gathered together. It must have been magnificent to see all those sails flying with the wings of the Opera House behind them. The Captain wanted to stop for coffee, so we plunked down at a small table in the sun outside a café that specialized in Belgian chocolate. The mocha I ordered was the most delicious thing I had tasted in a month, and there was one exquisite white chocolate truffle for each of us. The Captain called it "first aid," and indeed if felt like it.

On we went, and the day just became more and more amazing to me – here in Australia, on the other side of the world, in the company of two beefy, *machista* Balkan sailors! Even the seagulls, waddling aggressively around the esplanade on their bright orange feet, seemed part of the magic. All I could do was go with the flow. Karlo found the monument, a beautiful frieze in yellow stone, each of its three sides representing one phase of Australia's colonial development – first soldiers, then prisoners, and finally families. There were real leg irons and a chain embedded in the middle one. Then we went in search of the Italian restaurant he remembered, but it was closed, so we settled on an outdoor grill under awnings, cool but still

70

in the sun. The Captain ordered an aged rib-eye, Karlo the kangaroo steak, and I had something called a "Cesar salad chicken wrap," that showed up with shaved Parmesan cheese and big slices of prosciutto with a lovely glass of Chardonnay. Karlo leaned away from his plate and took a picture of his kangaroo steak.

As the Captain likes to tell stories of the kind that make you wide-eyed, either with fear or incredulity, many of which involve his being in danger, snake bites and poison arrows figured largely in our luncheon conversation. So in a break in what was mostly a monologue, I told them how I find myself feeling every time we leave port, this kind of giddy joy at returning to sea, almost like a homecoming, and I asked them if they ever felt that. "No," Karlo said, "It's just a job to us now."

"What a shame," said I – not in any judgmental way, I sincerely meant it. Later in the lounge Karlo admitted to having had similar feelings when he was a cadet, sitting in the bow with nothing out there but sea and sky. Now he lives in the engine room and sees little of either. I could understand how that could sour a person. If the Captain ever had such feelings, he didn't say. I think he likes the stress, the danger, the adrenaline rush, but most especially the power of being completely his own man.

The lunch service had been slow, it was a long walk back to our rendezvous, time was getting short, and the Captain wanted to stop and get ice cream. After we paid the bill, I dashed into the ladies' room, and when I came outside I couldn't see them, so I walked back in the direction of the Opera House looking at every ice cream stand along the way. We had lost each other. I was just coming to the roundabout in front of the Opera House, when the Bosun hailed me from the waterfront loaded down with shopping bags. He was standing with Cristi, who, after settling into her hotel, was taking a stroll along the harbor. At that point I was worried that the Captain and Chief were still on the other side trying to find me, so the Bosun went off to get them. Cristi and I had yet another chance to say goodbye to each other, amazed that we had run into each other, and when the Bosun returned he spied our two officers across the street. We piled into the van, all of us in high spirits in spite of the confusion, and Sister Mary whisked us back to the port. I told her how grateful I was that she had come aboard the ship. In the shuttle I thanked the Captain and the Chief for a truly lovely day. As we mounted the accommodation ladder, we saw a double rainbow. A perfect ending.

Day Twenty-six, at Sea: Nineteen miles off the coast, heading south-southwest in a calm sea, in the lee of the landmass of Australia. I had a call from Third Mate around ten o'clock asking me if I wanted to see whales. I grabbed my camera and bounded up to the Bridge. There were hundreds of pilot whales around the ship, apparently migrating to the Indian Ocean to breed, but all I could see was lots of roiled water with a few spouts here and there. They were intent on moving, not playing, although I did see one or two break the surface – their long shiny backs curving so gracefully out of the water – and I saw one sound and flap its tail in the air. According to the Captain, they will be with us all day. Even if not visible, it's wonderful to know they're accompanying us south!

Always one to look at the dark side, the Captain said the Japanese would pay millions of dollars to have access to these waters for whaling, but fortunately the area is protected. He said that, in spite of the International Whaling Commission, whaling is still big business, and the Japanese fleet alone includes 2,000 factory vessels, each as big as 100 meters in length. He said we'll see whaling ships between New Zealand and Panama – they're all over the Atlantic and the Pacific, and they turn off their AIS so as not to be identified by other shipping, but everyone knows what they are.

Then he told a story about how a previous ship he was Master in had hit and killed a whale off Cape Horn. He said the whales' sonar is far better than anything humans have been able to come up with, so he speculated that the whale was old or sick or already injured. The whole ship shuddered when it hit. He slowed and turned the vessel into a wide circle to come back and see what had happened. The whale had been badly cut up by the propeller and was still alive when a number of great white sharks appeared and started feeding on it before it died. I find such stories unutterably sad. I have heard whales singing beneath the surface of the sea, and I can't imagine how anyone could kill such magnificent creatures.

Once on this sad tack, the Captain went on to talk about the porpoise meat being packed with the tuna in the processing plants of Portugal and Spain. "You open the can, how can you tell the difference?" He said in Limón, on the Costa Rican coast, you could buy porpoise fresh on the docks – also turtle. He guesses the same is true in our Pacific port of Puntarenas. I will have to ask Henry, the guy who comes up to the lake every couple of weeks with fish fresh off the Puntarenas boats. Occasionally the United States bans Costa Rican tuna for violations of the so-called dolphin-friendly fishing practices established by international treaty. They send inspectors to the docks to check the catch and if they find too many porpoises in the tuna boat holds, the fishermen have to clean up their act until the U.S. eventually accepts our exports again. It sounds like a losing battle.

Early in our voyage together, Cristi told me about the invariable seating arrangements at the passengers' table. She had boarded in Rotterdam with a guest captain of the line, who sat in the spot exactly perpendicular to the officers' table, with Cristi on his left. He was quite pleasant with Cristi, full of good stories and conversation. Aside from acknowledging their presence with a "Good afternoon, good appetite," the officers of the *Louise* entered the room and took their assigned seats and ignored Cristi entirely. She was fascinated by this bit of behavior. When the guest captain disembarked, she found herself moved to the perpendicular seat facing the officers, who continued to speak only in Serbo-Croatian and ignore her.

In New York, Lila came on board, and Cristi was saved. And eventually, one by one, she met the officers from Europe (the Filipinos having long since been kind to her). When I joined the ship in Manzanillo, I understood that the officers and crew were very busy, not only with the lading, but also the preparations for the transit of the Canal. Only Chief Engineer came up to F Deck to introduce himself while we were cruising through Gatún Lake. At lunch that day, the Captain came into the Mess without introducing himself. The others joined him, and Serbo-Croatian was the order of the day. I whispered to Cristi, "Is that the Captain?" and she giggled yes, and told me the whole story. Later that afternoon when Third Mate Denny took me on tour, we found the Captain in his office staring at his computer screen, and I stepped forward, extending my hand, and said, "Excuse me, Captain, I'm your new passenger. It's a pleasure to meet you." To his credit, he jumped up from his chair and shook my hand and made pleasant conversation for several minutes until Denny and I continued our tour. At meals, however, the pattern continued the same. With three of us at the passenger table we were in no want of any additional stimulus, so we ignored them too.

The night before their disembarkation in Sydney, Cristi expressed her curiosity about where I might be seated when she and Lila were gone. Given the available evidence, we were ready to bet it would be in her seat, the one facing the officers' table, and I said I would write to let her know. Lila hadn't been in on our earlier conversation about this, so she was intrigued and the next thing we knew she was asking Manny where he was going to put me in the morning. Manny thought it was a trick question, so he pointed to exactly where I was sitting, on an axis parallel to the officers' table. The experiment had been blown. "But then I wouldn't have the view," I reminded Manny, as I'd been sitting with my back to the portholes for over three weeks.

Cristi and Lila left in the morning, I had lunch with the Captain and Chief in Sydney, so that evening was my first solo performance at the passengers' table, now seated opposite to where I had been and with a nice view of the dark. In the three of them marched – "Good evening, good appetite" – even though we had just been having a convivial time in the lounge across the hall – and their conversation resumed in Serbo-Croatian. The only attempt the Captain made to include me was his question in English: "Are you lonely over there?" I assured him I was not.

At lunch the next day, Karlo came in before the others, and we had quite a lot of pleasant cross-table talk until the others arrived.

Finally, at dinner, I'd had enough and I brought my crossword puzzle book, on which I focused intently as I ate, not looking up at them even once. It seemed their talk was louder and more boisterous than usual. While an unlovely language to listen to, Serbo-Croatian seems to be very expressive, with many hand gestures and emphatic remarks, so the performance at the other table was quite lively. Finally, while I was slowly eating my peach slices, head still bent over my book, they left in a body and went back across the hall. "See you later," Karlo mumbled. "Hmmm," said I.

It seems there are men on the planet whose mothers never taught them good manners.

And I've finally had it with the diet, too. The Captain's preferences dictate the cuisine in the Officers' Mess, and he's strictly a meat and potatoes guy, the more meat the better. The culinary offerings reached a new nadir last night with the stewed pork neck. I ate little, but it didn't sit well with me for hours after. When the others had left the room, I asked Manny if I could eat what the crew eats. He seemed to think it would be possible at lunchtimes. I hope so. From what little I've seen, Ernesto is a mean Asian cook. It occurs to me that one of the reasons the Filipino officers eat with the crew is that they prefer the food!

A little after noon today I saw Point Howe off our starboard bow, a huge sandy cape which on the charts marks the southeast corner of

Australia. From there we turned almost directly west to pass between Tasmania and the south coast. Second Mate Enrique and I looked at a number of charts when I went up to the Bridge to see how things were going. We were headed into a squall, a dead white curtain hanging directly in front of us. Actual wind speed (including the ship's speed) was almost 40 knots. It had driven me off starboard E Deck, and it was *cold*. Enrique and I talked about our home countries. "Do they have mangos where you live?" he asked me. "Oh, yes, the fruit of the gods," I said. He pulled out a world chart and we were both pleased to discover that the Philippines and Costa Rica are at almost the same latitude. He pointed to the islands where we have been, and I noted that Fiji is almost due south of Tuvalu. I told him the story about the Tuvalu Government Council meeting underwater to dramatize the plight of their sandy island nation as the oceans rise. He hadn't heard that, but he knows that in many places in the Pacific rising seas will soon create a lot of refugees. "But you don't have to worry," he smiled, "You live in the highlands."

"And do you live on the coast?"

"No, I live in the highlands too."

Day Twenty-seven, Melbourne: Passing the headlands and the lighthouse under battens of gray cloud, the sea oily calm, we make the slow approach to Melbourne. The sun is rising later and setting earlier – this morning at 6:55 when I looked at the clock, it was still dark under the slate-colored clouds that we've been steaming under most of the morning. Last evening I noted that sunset now happens before 5:00.

I was interested in the relative size of the ports, how many ships they can take a day. The Captain said Melbourne can take 25 to 30, compared to Botany Bay's eight to 12. A pilot might personally bring in two or three in a day, with plenty of rest in between. I can imagine it's a stress-filled job. I asked about the trickiest port we've seen so far, thinking that surely it was Noumea, but no: it's Tahiti. There are only four ship-lengths between the passage across the reef and the sharp left turn into the tiny harbor. In the soft pre-dawn light I had missed all that excitement! I've asked the Captain if I can be present on the Bridge during what they all call "maneuvers," and he said it's against the rules but that, if I stay out of the way on the port side, I can watch. This will be my first chance to see a pilot in action, although the Captain insists he alone is responsible for the maneuvering of the ship and the pilot is there only to advise.

The fog settled down on us like a giant's white feather bed, and seemingly as thick. The port has been closed. No ships are going out, no ships coming in. We are the only ship in the channel, proceeding at dead-slow speed, pilot on board. We can see nothing on either side. On deck, it doesn't feel especially cold; there is no wind and barely a ripple along our hull. It feels as if time itself has stopped.

We plowed slowly ahead through what seemed an interminable, blind passage, and finally – the channel narrowing dramatically and the fog lifting for just a few moments – we could see the towers of downtown Melbourne draped in gauze. Port Phillip is a big bay, 40 miles long and 20 across, so even in good weather it would be difficult to see from one side to the other. From what little I saw, it wasn't a pretty approach, along the shore mostly industrial sprawl. A last we docked only an hour behind schedule, the word "schedule" a fleeting concept at sea. What I've learned to pay attention to is not the printed schedule we were given when coming on board, nor even the Company's web site, that, according to those who have seen it recently, now seems sadly out of date; what the Captain says is what usually goes . . . within hours, if not minutes. The closer we get to a destination doesn't necessarily guarantee more accuracy, however – our forced drifting off Sydney, the need to drop anchor briefly in Noumea to wait for another ship to vacate our berth, the dense fog here in Melbourne are good examples of the unpredicted. The printed schedule says we were to depart Melbourne late at night on the 21st. We docked at 3:00 p.m. on the 22nd. Who knows when we will arrive in Napier, our next port? The Captain's constant reminders of the uncertainties at sea are philosophical. Eventually, one stops asking "when" questions. We are not in control.

Given the weather conditions, I decided against going up to the Bridge to watch the final maneuvering into the dock. It amuses me how, in just a month on board, I have absorbed some of the crew's fear of upsetting the Captain. People don't exactly kowtow to him, but I notice they tread lightly, and with an almost exaggerated respect. He rules not by virtue of his position alone, but also his temper.

Also because of the weather – a freezing rain – I decided to stay on board. It was late in the day, the port was huge and forbidding, and even a trip with some of the crew to the Seaman's Center to use the Internet failed to appeal. And I might have missed the pork bellies for dinner! After my conversation with Manny about the "cuisine" in the Mess, he understood when I asked him to leave the meat off my plate, and he asked me if I would like to try some green beans Filipino-style. They, the sauerkraut and potatoes made up my dinner, while our two new passengers went after the pork bellies with apparent gusto. I've never even heard of a pork belly – or is that what they trade on the Chicago Mercantile Exchange?

The new passengers came on board an hour or so after we docked, and we met in the passageway as I was going below to the Officers' Lounge before dinner. Hearty handshakes, pleasant manners, both with a sense of humor. Ian, the younger (a bit older than I am) is writing a book, and this is his fourth freighter voyage. Charles, in his mid-seventies, too is an ocean voyager, and both of them will have circumnavigated the globe when they terminate this trip in Tilbury-on-Thames. Neither of their spouses enjoys this kind of travel, and so Ian's wife will fly to England to join him. I told them that Roger had said he would be bored for 49 days at sea. So that puts us all in the same boat, so to speak.

I was pleased to have the chance to introduce both the new passengers to the Captain, the Chief Engineer, the electrician and Manny in the lounge before dinner. Since nobody introduced *me* to any of these people, I feel I have made up for a large gap in the social niceties on board ship. (Igor, the electrician, even thanked me.) They both joined me for a drink, and I'm delighted to say neither of them smokes. Ian seems up for table tennis, which should be amusing crossing the Tasman Sea – where will the ball really go? Perhaps I can interest them both in the word game a friend gave me to entertain everybody.

So, we seem to be off to a swimming start, and it will be fun observing how the new members of our little family alter the social dynamics on the *Louise* for the next 22 days.

Passage Five
Australia to New Zealand
The Birthday Party

Day Twenty-eight, at Sea: Departed Melbourne at nine in the morning, while I was doing my yoga, trying to do all the standing poses I can't do on the high sea. Unbending at the end of a sun salutation, I noticed that my right porthole is unblocked – I now have a view! Up to now there have been containers piled up within a couple of meters of my cabin, allowing me only a partial view to port. Maybe the Captain wants me to have a clear angle to take pictures of the seven-meter seas crashing over the foredeck that he keeps saying we're going to run into.

There was a strange new container-moving vehicle in the port at Melbourne that I am almost at a loss to describe. Imagine two steel bars sitting on eight rubber tires in two parallel rows. From each of the four corners rises a stilt – I don't know what else to call it – that, all together, support an oblong frame exactly at a height to permit this thing to pass *over* a stack two containers high. Mounted on the upper frame is whatever machinery is needed to propel the vehicle, along with a drop-down lift. Perched on the front (which could also be the back, depending on what direction it is scooting in) hangs a glassed-in control cage for the operator. In Melbourne, instead of abutting each other, the containers are stacked with skinny alleys between them exactly the width of each side of this Martian-looking machine. It slips into the alleys, glides over a stack, locks onto and lifts up the top container and scoots around to the side of the ship, where it lowers the box onto a frame, from which the gantry crane can scoop it up. It seemed there were hundreds of these beasts dashing around last night, all lit up, and hooting at each other like gangly prehistoric birds. I am constantly fascinated by the minds that dream up this stuff.

After lunch Third Mate Denny gave a safety orientation to the new passengers, and I asked if I could join them to take pictures of his immersion suit demonstration. This was great fun for everyone, until Denny said there was no more going up on the Bridge without permission. "Does that mean we can *ask* for permission?" I asked, but I don't think he understood me because he just repeated, "Captain's new order, no going on Bridge without permission." We were all disappointed, but even more, I felt a pang of guilt. Just the night before I had gone up to the Bridge with my computer to see if I could pick up a stray wi-fi signal, and I had been there no more than five minutes without success. Denny had even told me I could go. But I ran into the Captain on the way down the stairs, my computer under my arm, and he may have drawn his own conclusions. The Bridge is necessarily a secure area – there are microphones all over the place, so there are surely multiple ways to detect if anyone comes up there.

What interested me about my reaction was that it was so childish. No one has told me not to go to the Bridge without permission, but I felt guilty for having broken a rule even though I hadn't known it was a rule. I also felt just a twinge of teariness at the back of my throat at what seemed to me the arbitrariness of the Captain's decision. I wondered if he was angry, if I had done other things to aggravate him, if I could in any way appease him; I assumed there was no appeal. It felt as if the others were being punished because of me and that we were all being treated unfairly.

This was so directly out of my "father script" that I recovered my senses within a minute or two. Of course, the Captain's authoritarianism has been reminding me of Dad. He thought of himself as the Captain of his family and the more arbitrary he could be, the more unsettled and controllable the rest of us were. The very nature of arbitrariness is its unpredictability: it keeps people off-balance. By making them super-sensitive to the subtleties of pleasing or appeasing the tyrant, it asserts control over their behavior. It makes them afraid.

Now I need to ask myself to what degree am I reading my father's behavior into the Captain. Indeed, I haven't been making it all up. He has said to me on more than one occasion that he likes being the boss. In fact, at lunch in Sydney, he told me that the two most powerful job positions in the world are held by airplane pilots and ship captains – their authority is absolute, nobody argues with them. He's been offered a job at Fleet Navigation Control at the Head Office, but he's loath to take it. On the bridge of a ship, he's his own man, he gives the orders, people do what he says. In an office – even if he were running it – he'd be at least partially subject to the needs of others, and his time wouldn't always be his own.

So it shouldn't surprise me that I've identified in him some of the traits of the strongest authoritarian figure in my own life. I wonder how many other people this happens to on board ship? How vulnerable we are! Goebbels had it right: you can control anybody if you keep them afraid enough.

Day Twenty-nine, at Sea: At sundown yesterday we passed through Bass Strait between Tasmania and Australia. According to Ian, from the beginning of European settlement there was a lot of traffic between the island and the mainland, but there were so many forbidding rocks and shoals that for a long time it wasn't known that the Strait was navigable, and it was first explored only in small boats. The light from the setting sun behind us threw a pink glow on the lonely mound known as Redondo, a huge round rock sticking straight up out of the silvery sea like a blob of cookie dough on a baking sheet. There was a tanker off to port, also bound for the Strait, and the setting sun turned the back of her super-structure from white to bright red.

We're heading easterly at last. We've turned the corner. I'm headed home.

We've started to take back our time zones, like a little Pac-man creature turning and gobbling up its fellows behind him. This morning, it wasn't just dark when I woke up, it was dark most of the way through breakfast, and only when I went out on the sloshy deck at 7:30 was the sky beginning to lighten under clouds and sea a gunmetal gray. When I looked out the porthole at 6:30, the stars had seemed as big as lollipops, and the big black cloud on the eastern horizon was plainly outlined by starlight alone. I thought, "Weather ahead," but what do I know? All I know how to recognize is a squall line. We've had so many warnings about the roughness we're to expect in the Tasman Sea (what the Aussies and the Kiwis call "The Ditch") that I find myself looking forward to it . . . and looking forward . . . and it's still not happening. The *Louise* is just yawing along as usual.

First Mate has also warned that temperatures will be lower in New Zealand. It's farther south. The exterior temperature when we left Melbourne was 12C. In my cabin it hovers between 21 and 22. I asked Charles if he remembered how to convert Celsius to Fahrenheit, and he said all he remembered was that 38C is equal to 100F, and that normally a heated house in winter is maintained at 25C or so. That's a lot warmer than 21. Last night at dinner, wrapped up in a sweater and a huge woolen shawl, I kept rubbing the end of my nose to warm it up!

Our other passengers are two very interesting fellows. Charles was a career Australian Navy chaplain and he's been all over the Pacific and Indian Oceans. He said he would like to have gone on, but compulsory retirement age was 52. He then had a land-based congregation for many years. This is his second freighter voyage. From harumphy he grows expansive over a glass of whiskey.

Ian's on his fourth freighter voyage but has also traveled extensively by train all across China, Russia, Europe and the Near East, including on the Trans-Siberian Railway. We sat in the E Deck lounge over tea and coffee in the afternoon, both of us having a hard time taking our eyes off the wall map, as he traced his many voyages, and as we talked about the incredible romance of travel on trains and ships. Planes don't offer anywhere near the same experience, unless it's a small craft and you can see the "map" below you . . . otherwise, you're just sitting in a hermetically sealed tube with a lot of people coughing and sneezing. I told him about that particular thrill I feel every time we put to sea, and we agreed: it's about the sea, it's about the movement of the train across the rails; it's not especially about the places you pass by along the way.

He recounted the story told by turn-of-the-century seafarer Joshua Slocum, who, after retiring from the command of a clipper ship, rigged himself up in a small sailboat and circumnavigated the globe. Stopping in South Africa and visiting friends in the interior, he found himself dining with a Protestant missionary who was still convinced that the Earth was flat. Ian said Slocum's book about his voyage was fascinating reading. I can well imagine. Listening to him talk about his travels, I feel as if I've fallen into a sub-set of humankind that I always suspected was there but never knew I was secretly a member of. And I wonder if I would do this again.

After lunch, I went out on the port side – now the north side of the ship – to enjoy the sunlight. It was bright enough out of the wind that I was almost tempted to go in and fetch my folding chair. I peeked around the corner, however, and saw a squall line charging our bow, so I just stood at the rail, face upturned to the warmth, and basked in it for a quarter of an hour. The sea, aside from that easy quartering roll on the starboard bow, was like Mona's "swimming pool."

Third Mate Denny came around with our Saturday Slop Chest orders, and then I gathered my courage and called the Bridge. It seems I'm elected to interface with the Captain in cases of uncertainty because I've known him longer. Both the other passengers have picked up a little trepidation from the crew members, I think. Charles, for example, was under the impression that he couldn't go outside at all, when the only deck prohibition applies to Main, because it's a working deck. Second Mate was on the Bridge, and I asked if we could come up to look at the charts. He put me on hold and asked the Captain, who was right there, then came back on the line and said to come up. This was good news. It meant to me that the Captain was willing to be gracious now that he has established the ground rules.

I rounded up the others and we had a congenial little visit above, looking over the charts for Melbourne, Cook Strait between North and South Islands of New Zealand, and then the route north up to Napier on the east coast. The Captain told us that Second Mate was being promoted to First in four days – it was a real pleasure to shake Enrique's hand in congratulations; this is an important step for him. His shoulders seemed to ride a little higher, and there was a new tone of authority in his voice. The current First Mate will be leaving us in Napier.

So all is well. We came back downstairs and made ourselves some tea and chatted for a little about "home" things. Then I went back out on the port side for a last look at the day. At four o'clock, it was no longer warm, but the sea reflected the slanting rays of the sun like a field of diamonds.

Day Thirty, at Sea: The "where am I?" moments keep flying at me. Last night I found myself explaining the rules of American football to an Australian Anglican priest in the lounge – perhaps not so strange in itself, but on board a container ship crossing the Tasman Sea, with a 15 knot wind blowing at us straight off Antarctica (there being nothing between us and there)? There was another moment at dinner, when we were discussing Tudor history and Karen Armstrong's *The History of God,* and trying to remember Queen Elizabeth's wonderful "I have the heart and stomach of a king." I am continually struck by the human connections possible across such divides of culture, time and geography. I smile inwardly in gratitude, although I realize my past limits my ability to interpret such moments because they bear no relation to anything known or familiar. In fact, they jerk me out of my accustomed self and into a new place filled with new ideas, new appreciation of others, the joy of discovery and an exquisitely heightened sense of connectedness. We all really are in the same boat. I must never take that idea for granted, nor forget to cherish this new receptivity to life.

Looking out my porthole later, I see only the open sea, with five ports of call behind us, an almost full moon in the pure bowl of the sky casting its silver lights on the small waves at our hull. There are few clouds, and what stars are visible are dimmed by the brilliance of the moon. Outside the glass of the port, which fogs with my breath, the cold magic quickens. It looks like a winter's night.

Day Thirty-one, at Sea: *I have been learning how to deal with pain, or perhaps it would be more accurate to say that I am finding an adaptation to this new environment. My neck doesn't bother me nearly as much, and when it does I simply lie down flat, sometimes listening to music, sometimes not. Whichever, I probably spend a couple of hours during the course of the day simply resting. With that particular panic under control, the rest of me seems to hurt less (my fingers hurt from typing, so I don't spend as much time doing that either), and I'm generally sleeping well, albeit always with a pill. To some degree, I have been able to put some distance between myself and all the worries that were plaguing me at home. It's a lot easier to shut the door against them when they're thousands of miles away. Even with Roger, having resolved at least to try to open things up between us, I feel less fearful. I haven't stopped wanting, though. But wanting affection, wanting tenderness shouldn't be such an unreasonable desire! Even expressing those wants makes the self-pity start to burn behind my eyelids, and I remember that the wanting goes far deeper than just Roger, and that it has far more to do with my own, old miseries than with any other human being.*

The day dawned dark and squally. Sunrise was only a brief smoldering fire on the horizon, quickly damped down by the heavy clouds. Later today we'll be passing through Cook Strait before turning northward toward Napier. Ian said that Captain Cook got his start charting along the northern coasts of the Americas, and that some of his charts of eastern Newfoundland are still in use. What an amazing generation of men – all those explorers and adventurers left their marks all over the planet. Do you suppose that's why they did it? Was it just the 16th century equivalent of seeing their names in lights?

Night before last, the phone rang me out of a sound sleep about 9:30. The Filipino voice said, "Sandra."

"Yes?"

"We want you to come to the party." There was no doubt about which party he meant; the crew and Filipino officers had been going at the karaoke since before dinner. I had been shanghaied into one of these affairs my first night on board but only stayed for a few minutes. Likewise, when Denny celebrated his birthday, Cristi, Lila and I all attended to sing along for the length of time we considered polite, and no more. The noise level in the Crew's Lounge is always excruciating, so there's no incentive to stay. This time it was apparent that the crew was being given a chance to let off a little steam after all the hard work in the Australian ports, and it was Third Engineer's birthday. Something – God knows what – induced me to say yes. Maybe I thought I was still dreaming. "I'll be there in a few minutes," I said.

"Why so long?" the voice asked.

"I was asleep. I need to get dressed."

Then the incredible question, "Are you naked?" I was dumbstruck. "Are you naked?" the voice repeated. What was this, a Filipino phone-sex call in the middle of the Tasman Sea? How do I react? All I could think to do was play it absolutely straight, so I answered, "No."

"Are you in your nighties?"

That was certainly the moment to end the conversation. "Goodbye," I said and then hung up, threw on jeans and a sweater, grabbed the can of Pringles I had just bought from the Slop Chest, and went downstairs. If I had sensed any danger at all, I would have locked my door and stayed on E Deck. But instead I was giggling. I thought the guys must have been well on their way to a grand drunk, because I couldn't think of a single member of the crew or any of the officers who had ever treated me other than with respect, even deference. I am old enough to be their mother, for Heaven's sake! Perhaps it was just curiosity that drove me. I thought I had recognized the voice, but I won't embarrass him now by using his name. And I figured that, with any luck, he would forget all about it by morning.

The party had degenerated to the silly stage by the time I got there, all of them joining in on the karaoke choruses, clapping riotously at the end of every performance, and jumping up and down in general hilarity. When

I opened the door, First Mate was balancing himself in his stocking feet on an upholstered chair and bellowing "My Way" into the microphone in good voice. I was relieved to see that both the electrician and Chief Engineer – whose son's 18th birthday it was also – had already joined the party, and I was given a seat at their table along with a glass of wine. Everybody sounded glad to see me, and whoever had made the call didn't welcome me any more heartily than the rest. Pretty soon I suggested to Karlo that we start the dancing, and then all of them joined in, bouncing around the middle of the floor in various stages of inebriation. At one point I found myself dancing with a crew member who was weaving back and forth, waving his arms hula-style with his eyes tightly shut. Even Manny and I jitter-bugged a bit. Not too long after, and one by one, the crew began to drift off to their cabins and only Bosun was left on the sofa, head rolling from side to side with the motion of the ship, and Igor and one or two others still bouncing around to the music. The festivities obviously drawing to a close, Chief Engineer saw me safely to my cabin door. I haven't had that much fun in a long time!

Two days running now, I've been able to warm myself out on the sunny deck in the lee on the port side. This morning's cloudy beginning yielded to a perfect, brilliant day, the sea like a bathtub, not a speck of foam except what's churned up by our bow wave, the sky at its zenith the same indigo blue as the sea. We're entering Cook Strait, with the white cliffs of South Island on our right, the shadowy mountains peeking out over a misty bank of gray. Nothing of North Island yet. The Captain predicted we would be going through the narrows later in the afternoon. I stand out there at the rail, facing the sun and the sea, all by myself with the whole world for company.

Day Thirty-two, Napier, New Zealand: Or, rather, just the wide Hawke's Bay in front of Napier. It's been quite exciting speculating about all the schedule changes in the last twelve hours. The Captain told us yesterday afternoon that, because of a heavy swell at Napier left over from the recent storm that swept through from the south, the ship in front of us still hadn't been able to dock and unload her cargo. The port at Napier faces east and is not as sheltered from the Pacific as the other ports we've visited. The Captain said we would have to wait, either anchored in one of only two possible anchorages, or drifting, as we did off Sydney. So, we were all preparing ourselves for a long evening. Then at nine o'clock, a minion from the engine room found us chatting in the lounge after dinner, and told the Chief Engineer to call the Bridge. No, we were heading for Tauranga instead, pedal to the metal, as Karlo said, and full speed ahead. His take on the situation, looking at his watch, was that all the bean counters had showed up at the Head Office (exactly 12 hours from where we are) and they had decided the Company could save money by switching our itinerary around.

So this morning when I went on deck at 6:30, the moon a translucent disk in a pellucid sky, the eastern horizon blood-red and cloudless, I was convinced we were still full-ahead for Tauranga, where we were expected to dock around six this evening. This shift had been a disappointment because I had hoped to visit the hot springs there, and now we would be loading all night and getting under way in the morning for our return to Napier.

But no. While we were having our morning omelets, the Chief Engineer barged in for his "Balkan breakfast" – black coffee and a cigarette – and said, "Guess what? An hour later those guys at Head Office changed their minds." Out on deck a few minutes later, what to my wondering eyes appeared but Napier, white buildings stretched out along a low coast in a broad bay between limestone cliffs, a brisk wind whipping up little white caps in the chill, teal-colored water. The bean counters had decided that the load we would be taking on at Tauranga would deepen our draft to the point where we wouldn't be able to get *in* to Napier. (We're already running with no ballast except the fuel.) Good thing those guys are paying attention to this stuff. But it seems we will still have a day of waiting . . . and, of course, the Captain has dire predictions for the weather, which at the moment is clear and bright, if a little too cold for sunning on deck.

And finally, there we were, pulled up to the dock and entertaining the Immigration and Customs officials by two o'clock. Released on shore, we three passengers waited at the gangway with the port agent for the jitney bus to come around and get us. We were not even allowed to touch our feet on New Zealand soil until the bus had arrived. It was cold waiting there! The port agent said the Filipino crewmen suffer from the New Zealand temperatures too. He was a very pleasant, toothy fellow who welcomed us to his native land, and then had the kindness, once we were at last through the security gate, to drive us into Napier. As we were waiting, he said that the Company had telephoned to apply the necessary pressure to speed up our port entry. It seems that, with a ship coming into Napier every two weeks, the Company was able to exercise some pull.

Once in town, Charles, Ian and I went first to change money – they accepted not only my Australian but my Fijian dollars – and then agreed to meet at Divine's Coffee Shop after we'd done our errands. After some walking around, I found an Internet café that charged a dollar for every ten minutes. Having already paid six for a small bag of cashews to contribute to the Officers' Lounge, I was left with only four, which just scraped me through answering the mail. Nobody had heard from me since New Caledonia, so there was a lot to catch up on, and I walked away having forgotten a few notes that I'd wanted to send. I was aware that it was probably my last opportunity, too, until we hit Panama, since we'll be loading in Tauranga during the night.

We had a nice mocha at the coffee shop (not as good as the one in Sydney), and then I trundled off to find a taxi (having to change just a little more money first) to take me back to the ship. Ian and Charles were hankering after a real pub dinner.

Napier was leveled in an earthquake in 1931 and completely rebuilt in what looks like late 20s Art Deco. This is its one claim to fame, and it takes advantage of it, with bricked pedestrian malls, traffic lights that chirp at you, quaint store-fronts, helpful people, and not a poster, dirty-faced child, gum-wrapper, not even one Maori, *nada,* visible to the tourist eye. Jaywalking is illegal, but I did it anyway. "Well, I come from Costa Rica," I imagined myself explaining to the local jaywalking police. During one of these illegal crossings, I was filmed by a camera van, a white crime control unit with four swiveling cameras perched on top. I found this somewhat sinister. It seems that the good people of Napier pay their taxes and tolerate no monkey-business. As "cute" as it was, the place seemed as sanitized as a theme park; it lacked real human charm. I wasn't sorry to get back to the ship.

There's been quite a lot of chat throughout the voyage about piracy. Apparently it's always been a fact of life in the South China Sea and the Sunda Strait between Sumatra and Java, but everyone agrees that now the problem is growing. Karlo described how they used to do it in Sunda. There are thousands of native boats in the Strait, most of them fishermen. The channel is narrow and, just as at Suez, any ship coming through is vulnerable. All the pirates had to do was string a 100-meter line between two fishing boats and thus "catch" the bow of a freighter, the inertia of the ship bringing the two small boats quickly to either side, where with grappling hooks the pirates could scramble on board.

But even though the problem was endemic in those waters, in its scale it was nothing compared to the kidnapping of ships on the high seas that is now occurring off Somalia. As many as 800 crew are in Somali hands, most of them from countries that, for whatever reason, haven't paid their ransom. We don't see much news about these lost men. Third Mate Denny said piracy was "big business," meaning there is big money bankrolling these bandits. They have mother ships with several "go-fast" feeder boats – armed to the teeth with all the latest technology – that can outrun anything on the ocean. Denny told me he'd heard from a former senior officer that his current ship was just entering the Gulf of Aden after transiting Suez and the Red Sea when they heard a "mayday." Fearing it was a decoy, the captain didn't answer it. The law of the sea has always been to help those in distress, but when your own ship and lives are at risk? Our Captain said if his ship was boarded he wouldn't offer any resistance. "What can I do facing down an AK-47?" he asked. It's hard to imagine this paragon of *machismo* would be passive in such a situation, but his first concern has to be the safety of everyone on the vessel.

In the lounge last night, I asked everybody what motivates men to go to sea. I got a number of interesting answers. At the simplest level, in what the world now so kindly calls "developing nations" (Myanmar?), a lot of people are attracted to the pay, which is relatively good, or they simply lack other economic opportunities. I think Manny falls into this category. On board ship it's not easy to spend your salary, so there's a nice chunk ready for you when you finally go ashore. Ian, who pointed out Sir Edmund Hillary's first "hill" on the coast of South Island yesterday, its snowy peak all pink in the sunset, said you go "because it's there." Others – the Captain would be a good example – like the freedom, the independence. The wide open sea gives some men the sense of that, even though they might be tied to a ship for many months at a time. Seamen work on contracts. At the end of the term, they're free to go home and stay as long as they want and sign on for another go whenever the money runs out. The Captain likes the extra time with his family. This freedom has to be weighed against the job insecurity, of course, but he says the world is not stamping out seamen the way it does steel ships. Karlo said a motivation for him when he was young was to see the world, but he admits also to having been captivated by the ocean itself, the *idea* of the ocean, its mystique or romance. Charles, the retired Navy chaplain, pointed out that to be at sea for long periods you have to be able to "live inside yourself," something that not many people know how to do. He suggested there might be a higher proportion of such people among mariners. Since he was spiritual counselor to many over a long career at sea, he should know this well, and no doubt knows how to do it himself.

I was reminded of one of my early visits to the Bridge when the Captain was there. I had stood at the window gazing out at the far horizon, the glittering ocean empty in all directions, and I said in an awed voice, "We're all alone out here."

"Yes," replied the Captain in the same quiet tone, "We are."

Living inside myself is not often easy, and the moments when I feel quiet within are rare enough to be cherished. (Entertaining myself, on the other hand, comes readily. That's one of the reasons I write.) After a bad night, I pushed myself through the morning exercise routine and then just lay down to rest my neck for an hour. At last my brain, tired of all its clamor through the long night, let go for a moment and I felt – or heard – another voice saying, "Accept the wanting."

Day Thirty-three, at Sea: We departed the dock during the night, and I was sleeping too soundly to notice. I went to bed interested to see what the weather would do, since my taxi driver had said there was a bad storm coming – 100-kilometer-an-hour winds, heavy rains. This morning, I think our worthy Captain has successfully outrun the weather once again. There was a heavy swell for a few hours, but now we're cruising calmly north along the east coast of North Island. Every time I go outside to look, it seems as if there's nothing much there.

Ian said that the Maori put up a much stiffer resistance to European settlement than did the Aborigines of Australia and that the population of New Zealand has always been relatively small. The Captain added that the European Union, with its restrictive trade policies, finished the country off, economically speaking. Finally, New Zealand is following its larger neighbor's example and turning its face to the Orient. As a result, trade is improving and tourism is taking hold.

At some point today we'll turn the corner and head westerly for Tauranga on the north coast, our last port of call before Panama. Part of me wants to go home, and part of me wants to stay out here on the ocean forever.

We'll be losing a few of our crew and gaining replacements in Tauranga. Several of the men had hoped to disembark in Sydney, but the Company "extended" their contracts until they could get replacements lined up. First Mate is one who will be leaving, Second Mate Enrique stepping up to fill his place, and ship's rumor has it that there will be a new Hungarian officer filling Enrique's role. This person, no doubt, will sit at the officers' table at meals, introducing a whole new element to our evening's entertainment. Somehow, I doubt that the new Second will speak Serbo-Croatian, and I'm pretty sure none of our existing officers speaks Hungarian, which means that the lingua franca of the Officers' Mess will now be English. And what seat will the new man take? Opposite the Captain at the foot of the table, or to the Captain's left? What fun!

We are just passing White Island, an active volcano in the Bay of Plenty that Charles has seen many times from navy destroyers. I had just happened to catch a glimpse of it out the porthole after lunch and ran to Charles's cabin to ask him if this was it. New First Officer Enrique said we could come up to the Bridge and check out our position and look at the island through the big binoculars. He said tourist ships stop there. Shades of home. Looking at the charts, you can see a number of submerged volcanoes developing in the immediate vicinity – just like the Galapagos, all part of the Ring of Fire. It would be interesting to look at the undersea geologic maps and trace the fault lines and volcanoes all the way to Costa Rica (although I think a large part of the ocean floor remains uncharted).

First Mate tells us we should be at the dock by 6:00 p.m. and that we'll start unloading pretty soon after. Probably the first thing to go will be the three-million-dollar yacht. This ought to be high entertainment, but if I want to see it I'll have to forego shore leave. I asked the Captain if he knew any good restaurants, but he shook his head sadly and said, "I wish." Tauranga is where he has to be especially vigilant about the weight of the cargo coming on board – all those frozen lamb chops – so he'll be keeping his eye on the draft all night.

Our last landfall. As we pushed slowly into the narrowing channel of Tauranga, the sun set red in a cloudless sky behind low hills overhanging the ice-blue water. A dark line of conifers profiled the shore. It could have been anywhere on the Atlantic coast of North America. I don't feel any particular need to go ashore. I'm comfortable on board, not at all hungry for the solid impress of land on the soles of my feet.

We took on provisions in Napier – fresh greens in the salad! Our poor Cook had abandoned even trying to offer his dispiriting assemblage of shredded white cabbage, the last browning innards of the iceberg lettuce, and currants. Nobody was bothering even to turn back the plastic wrap on the bowl to have a look. But today, since Ian didn't want any salad, I had a double helping. Perhaps I was getting a little Vitamin C-deprived. In Charles Dana's day, hailing an outbound ship off the coast of Brazil on their homeward run (*Two Years before the Mast*), his captain begged some fresh onions and potatoes. He had a couple of cases of scurvy on board. The crew had been so starved for anything fresh that they carried the onions around in their pockets so they could munch on them at will. I can appreciate that!

Day Thirty-four, at Sea: Ian and Charles went ashore last night to find another Irish pub dinner, and I'm glad I didn't go with them because the jitney never came from the gate to pick them up and they had to hitch a ride with the quarantine truck. Waiting in the bitter cold is not my idea of fun. However, Ian reports this morning that he saw a wonderful sign in the port, "Beware of the Straddles." This, then, is what you call those sci-fi monsters that were scuttling around in Melbourne, and now here – although these are higher – the ones that *straddle* the stacks of containers, pick them up and deliver them to the cranes . . . of course, why didn't I think of that? I got some pictures of them last night, with all the lights of the port blazing, and again this morning – another perfect, cloudless sapphire sky, against which the bright colors of the gantries and the ship's fixtures stand out like industrial jewels. It occurred to me that the straddles are probably much cheaper to run since they don't have to be heavy enough to provide a counterweight to the boxes they lift. I saw a woman operator in one of them, so it's not exclusively a men's world, this world of cargoes and ships.

I stayed on board last night to watch the unloading of the yacht, which the Captain had assured me would be one of the first things to come off. If it was, they just beamed it up to another planet because I never took my eyes off the foredeck for more than two minutes, from 5:30, when I saw the gantry operator take the little elevator up to his glass cage, to almost 9:30. I abandoned my dinner six times to run out on deck when I thought something was about to happen. At one point I dashed up to my cabin to get a jacket and hat, then up to F Deck, where the cold just bit through my hat, sweater, jacket, shawl and slacks, and where I could only stand for about five minutes before hurrying back inside to watch from the portholes in my cabin, then out again, and up, and down and up that damn ladder until finally I just gave up with exhaustion and the cold, and comforted myself with the fantasy that they wouldn't unload it till morning.

I've never been able to see the yacht from my cabin. In fact, it wasn't even visible from the Bridge. The only thing you could see was the "hole" in the containers, the obvious gap where it has been parked ever since it was boarded in Savannah. Last night I saw nothing going into or out of that gap, but this morning the yacht is no longer there. The hole is filled up with boxes, and I missed my photo. It would have been interesting. Nobody seemed to know if they were going to offload it directly into the water or onto a waiting truck. In either case, the crane would have needed different terminal tackle from the steel frame and paddles that it uses to pick up the containers. The yacht was *not* in a box. If I hadn't actually seen a tiny bit of its stern through the little hatch in the Main Deck on our tour to the bow, I might not believe it was really there.

The Captain showed up at lunch with someone we had never seen before, dressed in blue overalls and carrying a small pack. He sat on the Captain's right – the place of honor – and was offered a beer. With his ruddy cheeks and blonde hair, I assumed him to be our new Hungarian officer, just arrived; in fact, I was convinced of it because I couldn't understand a word he said. After a little while, however, it dawned on me that the Captain was speaking to him in English. And then I heard it: a pure tripthong-laden New Zealand accent! Later we learned that our guest was with Customs and that the new Second Officer is really Filipino.

We're losing time here in Tauranga. Yesterday, First Mate told us we were scheduled to be in port 14 hours, and that meant we would get away from the dock about 8:00. It's now 10:00. He said we were already a day behind. I asked if we could hurry up in port, and he said you can never hurry up in port – there are too many unpredictable factors in port, late deliveries, broken down cranes, a sick operator, an accident – and that the Captain would have to make up the time at sea. Now we're scheduled to leave at 2:00, even though the loading has long been finished. Other ships are coming in and we have to wait for traffic to clear in the channel. Maybe, as Karlo says, one of the other ships will be late and we can sneak out. Meanwhile, there's no shore leave, so we stare at the stacks of Radiata pine trunks on the dock, all perfectly round and all perfectly the same length, cultivated in vast forests just inland from here, and waiting for export to China and India. Even when they're farmed, dead trees make me a little sad. I'm ready to go. I'm not in a hurry to get anywhere; I just prefer to be at sea.

Somewhere I picked up the words *westerly, easterly,* etc., maybe from reading old seafaring novels. And I may have read them without having the least idea what the words really meant. When I use them now, I do it to indicate direction *to* a place, as in heading toward the west or east or whatever. But in Nautical-ese, this is true only if you're talking about the wind; if it's blowing *to* the east, it's an easterly breeze. If you're talking about the current, however, you have to shift your mental global positioning system; an easterly *current* is heading west. So an easterly current will slow you down if your sails are depending on an easterly breeze. I bet you always wanted to know that.

On ships you have two speeds: knots (that's nautical miles, but you never *say* "nautical miles," you say "knots" – one equals 1.15 statute miles) per hour in the water, and knots per hour over the ground. The latter is the true measure of the distance you are covering, since measuring the passage of the hull through the water doesn't take into account ocean currents that might be working against you. Before the invention of GPS, speed was always a relative thing until you got out your handy sextant and chronometer and you could see how far you had really traveled in a given period of time.

When we talk about wind and vessel speed, we use the word *knots*. When we talk about distance, we have to say *nautical miles,* shortened to "miles." I have no idea why all this nautical nomenclature has to be so confusing.

In over a month, there has only been one occasion when we had the wind at our back doing more knots than the ship. The Captain assures me this happens only rarely. It creates a vacuum in front of the superstructure that sucks engine fumes right into the air-conditioning intake, and this makes your cabin smell like the inside of a gasoline pump. I awoke to this one night and lay awake for quite a while wondering whether I should call somebody to tell them the ship would explode if anybody lighted a cigarette. I opened my porthole to let in some fresh air but, since my cabin faces forward, the air outside smelled the same as the air inside. Eventually I assumed that, if there really had been a problem, somebody would have sounded the alarm, and I went back to sleep.

A little before 2:00 p.m. our tugs arrived. The tug's bump against the hull is my signal to go out on deck and watch. Here in Tauranga we came into port under our own power, but we needed two tugs to push us against the dock. In leaving, we needed two tugs as well, one to keep our nose in position while the other towed our stern around 180 degrees until we were bow-first into the channel. Charles stood out on the port side with me and watched them maneuver. He recalled the days when tugs and ships used to communicate with their horns, like Morse code with toots. Now, of course, ships and tugs have all kinds of other communications and they don't need to sound their horns anymore. It took half an hour to pull us away from the dock and get us pointed in the right direction and, as the last tug retrieved her line and started away from our hull, we waved to the deck hand and he waved back. I turned to Charles and said, "Toot-toot." Next stop Panama.

Passage Six
New Zealand to Panama
The Captain's Ice Cream

Day Thirty-five, at Sea: This deep-throated beamy roll lasts just about the length of the passage along the cabins on E Deck. You start up hill at the port end, and about midway you find yourself heading back downhill to starboard. There's a bit of a yaw, so you also weave back and forth, touching the handrails for reassurance. The sea bears a few flecks of foam, the surface almost smooth, just this under-roll coming from somewhere far off, probably. No doubt the Captain will enlighten us at lunch about all the bad weather either ahead of or behind us. This morning the sun rose right through my cabin portholes, instantly warming the room. And the temperature on the sunny side is warmer – I've taken off my sweater and cracked open the port for a little fresh air. We're cruising east-northeast, and tonight we'll cross the International Dateline again and we'll have two Fridays. Does that mean I just go to sleep as usual and wake up to find that it's the day before all over again?

Leaving the land. I stand out on deck and watch the end of day, the shadow of the New Zealand coast growing dimmer with every mile. The last sight before facing the infinity of the empty ocean is White Island, its right flank coated a dusty mauve, a tiny plume of smoke and ash from its crater pure white against the darkening sky.

I see that my time is limited, shrinking instead of expanding, as it was when I faced the disappearing horizon west of the Americas. A small panic pricks my heart with the realization that I am still burdened with wanting something I'm not likely to get. I think, "I've got two weeks to come to terms with that." Then another little voice inside me pipes up and says, "Why?" I smile to myself. Yes, why not be the person I am? Why do I

97

have to come to terms with, atone for, bow and scrape to the old guilts and betrayals? I think the answer, finally, is that I don't.

Karlo and I have been talking in the lounge after dinner. He used to entertain Lila and Cristi over a glass of wine till all hours, but I wasn't interested in drinking after dinner and inhaling all their smoke, so I begged off. I don't know what he talked to them about, but Lila always seemed to be full of "Chief Engineer said this, Chief Engineer said that," usually things having to do with the ship or the voyage.

Karlo was the only officer to introduce himself to me while we were cruising through Gatún Lake. We stood in the sun and chatted at length, and I noticed he had questing eyes that looked right into yours in a way that implied an understanding, as if we both were in on a big, happy secret. It was not a hunting, but rather a kindly, look.

The next day when Denny was taking me around the ship, we passed the Chief Engineer's Day Room and Denny introduced us. Karlo grinned and stuck out his hand to give mine a hearty shake, as if we hadn't already met. "We met yesterday," I laughed, and I saw Denny flash Karlo a knowing look. Thus subtly are the signals between the sexes given and received. It was that same evening that I saw Karlo through the door of the Officers' Lounge when I was going in to dinner and he gave me that little lecture about the importance of being social at sea. So the next day I bought a bottle of Jack Daniels (the only thing passing for whiskey in the bonded store), and brought it down to the lounge and plunked it on the bar. He arrived seconds later with another bottle, and he said, "No need to have so many bottles here. These will not be yours or mine, they will be ours," and he stowed mine under the bar. And so the evening happy hour was born, and within a day or two the Captain started coming to the lounge before dinner to join in the conversation. In fact, he frequently took over the conversation with his funny stories, while Karlo would stand behind the bar with his arms crossed, puffing on his cigarette in frustration. They seemed to be competing for laughs, especially after Cristi and Lila joined us and our little gathering became even jollier. After Melbourne, it didn't take our new passengers more than a day to discover their only opportunity to socialize with the officers on board. Charles is adjusting to the bourbon.

The officers are not always there. When the ship is in maneuvers, or loading and unloading in port, they frequently miss meals altogether. I found I was missing the entertainment when they were not there, especially Karlo's. He did thoughtful little things – getting ice from the Galley, making up some non-skid coasters one day after my drink slid all the way

*to the end of the bar, keeping the lounge stocked with snacks. He even
makes sure the right glasses are in the rack. Once, after I began to
appreciate all these small gestures, I told him he was a thoughtful person.*

*Wouldn't it be difficult to refrain from fantasizing about a fling with
somebody who's so obviously trying to please? I found I looked forward
to seeing him, and if I didn't I would be disappointed. Sometimes we would
exchange complicit smiles over lunch or dinner. I would make up excuses
to step into the lounge where he was smoking after meals, just for a word
or two. Finally, a few days ago, I stepped in after dinner where he and
Igor were having a glass of wine, and they offered one to me. I accepted.
Igor quickly quitted the field. Over several evenings of this, we have talked
about history, politics, war and philosophical – and even personal – things.
He's not shy about mentioning his wife and children, but he never
complains about them, as some men would to draw your sympathy. He
thinks, reflects about experience, tries to fit things that happen into a
coherent system in his head, and he has developed a wide tolerance for the
different people he has encountered in his travels. He seems to appreciate
my conversation, so I feel valued.*

*I realized last night, however, that he's been using me as a
"confessor." He knows this is a short-term friendship, so he's
unburdening himself to a sympathetic somebody in a way he rarely can.
How many women travel alone on freighters? At the end, we'll go our
separate ways, anything said forgotten, no consequences worth fretting
over. I really don't think he has anything else in mind. His liking of me
has to do with the power that my attention has for* him, *not with any special
attraction in myself. So I have become the Sailor's Friend. Will this be the
final blow to my vanity? If I were younger or more courageous, I might try
to exact the price of a small tenderness.*

Last night's dinner conversation was a little more animated than
usual when Charles and Ian started talking about U.S. politics. When they
got around to the two Bush elections, Charles asked me what I thought of
Al Gore, and I said I thought he was a profoundly thoughtful and intelligent
man. Charles's response to that was to call Gore a liar. I shut immediately
up. He seems to have bought into the notion that Gore is exaggerating, or
even making up, all the climate change brouhaha for his own economic –
and probably political – gain. It's so awful when somebody makes a flat-
out, unsupported statement like that. I never have the wherewithal to
respond decisively; I just sat there tight-lipped with my eyes on my plate.

While I find Charles a bit cynical for a retired clergyman, up to now his views have seemed to be more in sympathy with my own, so this opinion of Gore took me by surprise. I shouldn't forget that, as an Australian native, he's probably reading "Uncle Rupert's" newspapers. It would be easy to just dismiss Charles, and stick to subjects on which we agree, but something nags at my innards. It didn't come up at lunch. We'll see if I have more courage when we meet before dinner.

Meanwhile, I am acutely aware that Ian had moved recently into Melbourne to escape the threat of bush fires – he showed us a photo of the property they had left behind, complete with swimming pool. He said they had viewed the pool as a "safety net" in case of fire. I said to Ian, "So you're an environmental refugee." He glumly agreed. According to Charles, the temperature on the ground when the bush spontaneously combusted in 2009 into multiple fires that claimed 22 lives was 47C (116.6F). Charles still lives in the country, but he and his wife take separate vacations because they're afraid to leave their property untended in case of fire. They have been busy over the last 15 years reforesting their acreage. What dots is he not connecting?

Charles is very knowledgeable about ships, naval history and even naval literature, so he is otherwise quite interesting to talk to. He wanted me to read *Billy Budd* next, which I am doing. Today over tea we have been talking about magnetic north and true north, and I learned that the former moves around over time, the latter is fixed, and the farther you are away from both, the greater the discrepancy. I'd like to learn more about why we need two norths, and why one of them isn't stationary! There's a lot to learn on a ship. This has been one of the unexpected pleasures of being at sea.

Finally, in a lull in today's dinner conversation, I turned to Charles and asked in as neutral a way as possible if he'd read any of Gore's books. He said no, and that he hadn't seen the movie either. I then suggested they might be worth reading, along with the reports from the Intergovernmental Panel on Climate Change and other scientific sources he could find readily on line. He agreed they would. Perhaps he had felt himself to be a little precipitate in his earlier statement. I'm glad he chose not to argue. End of that little conflict.

It's been interesting to hear from seasoned freighter voyagers about their previous experiences in other ships. Charles has been in a German ship, with German officers and Burmese crew, and he noted that English had been the only language in the Mess – or, in fact, anywhere in public – and that the passengers had been seated with the officers at meals. The food, however, was nowhere near as good as what he's enjoying on the *Louise* (I shudder to think!), and the Slop Chest was more limited in its offerings. He said it had run out of toothpaste just about the same time he did.

The language difference prompted me to ask Karlo one evening what things were like in other ships he has served in, and he made it clear that what we are experiencing here is unusual. The language was always English, no matter what the nationality of the officers and crew. In one ship he was the only European on board – everyone else was Burmese, including the captain, and the language was still English. I then asked him about the Filipino officers not taking meals in the Officers' Mess, and he said he was perturbed about this. He feels they have a right to be there, and allowing their absence – for whatever reasons – he considers slack management. He also confirmed my impression that frequently the conversation at the Captain's table centers on work, which he feels to be an infringement on his "relax time." After this little conversation, he leaned closer over the bar and said, "You know too much."

I laughed. "Knowledge is power!"

Day Thirty-five again, at Sea: Now, instead of being a day ahead of Costa Rica, I'm six hours behind.

We're still living with this deep swell and, with wind hitting our starboard bow, we're pitching and yawing, as well as rolling. I'm sure I've read the word *wallowing* in connection with ships – probably in a literary venue – but I'll happily nominate it for inclusion in the *Oxford Dictionary of Ships and the Sea* if it isn't already there. I offer the following definition: rolling around in every conceivable direction in the bottom of a trough. In such seas the bathroom becomes a big booby trap. The medicine chest is right over the sink, where you often find it, and its shelves, thoughtfully provided with two screwed-in stainless steel cup holders along with barriers across each shelf to keep things from falling out, are the only safe place to put anything down. The water glass, for instance. So you're brushing your teeth, lean over to spit out the toothpaste and come up to bang your head on the open medicine chest door. The shower is equipped with a single, small, vertically mounted grab-bar, just to the left of the water taps that jut out from the wall – all the stainless and brass pipes and connections are exposed – and you reach for it with shampoo in your eyes and find you have grabbed the searing hot water pipe instead. Washing your feet is a challenge because there's a lot of water sloshing back and forth with the roll of the ship and the tile is slippery. (Drain water has to be pumped out on a ship; gravity alone won't do it.) God forbid you should drop the soap. The shower curtain opens and closes of its own volition, and the only way you can fix it to the wall is when it's open.

But the worst trap, my nemesis, is the 20-centimeter-high-30-centimeter-wide doorsill you need to cross to get into the bathroom in the first place. There are sills like this in every area of the ship where you come into contact with water – between our tiny laundry room and the passage, between the passages and the decks, between the Galley and the Mess – and it's wonderful to see how people deal with this little obstacle. When the ship is really rolling, it's fun to watch Manny manage the service of a single bowl of soup, for example. (And his audience is usually in motion, our chairs sliding inexorably away from the table.) The most challenging time to deal with the bathroom sill is in the middle of the night. I quickly learned I had to turn on the light first (the switch thoughtfully placed *outside* the bathroom), because you could really kill yourself tripping over it in the dark. While almost all of my bruises have disappeared, the ones on the tops of my feet are nice and fresh.

The Captain says this swell is coming from the south, a big storm about 1,500 miles away and rolling east across the Southern Ocean to Cape Horn. In fact, we've altered our course to get farther away from it, 400 miles to the north of our preferred route. Right where we are at this moment, he said, in two days there will be a 300-mile-wide low pressure system with ten-meter waves and 60-knot winds. I remarked that it is really miraculous how we keep escaping the bad weather. Former Second Mate Enrique had shown me both possible routes from New Zealand on the chart a few weeks ago, a straight line and a curved line. He said the straight line – what we're now on – was longer, although on the flat chart it actually appeared shorter. It is a bit difficult to envision this, even though in my head I can understand how it would be true on a curved surface.

We passed another container ship today outbound from Panama to Auckland. I asked the Captain how many days off Panama she was: "Exactly the same number of days it will take us to reach Panama," he said. I had hoped I was being more subtle! He assures us we will be arriving in Manzanillo on August 12th. Whether the port has a ready berth for us when we get there, however, he won't hazard to guarantee.

Last night I saw the Balkan Peninsula. Both Igor and Karlo had responded to my wish of seeing their native countries with hundreds of photos that they displayed in the lounge on Karlo's laptop. In Igor's case, they were gleaned from the Internet, many of them touristy, some of them really stunning pictures in their own right. Karlo, whose English is far superior to Igor's, felt the need to comment on each one, which slowed things down some, and every time there was a picture of some fish – dead fish on the dock, dead fish in the market, dead fish on a plate – he felt the need to say, "More fish."

After Igor's collection, Karlo's was a geographically organized, as well as beautiful, presentation, including detailed charts of the eastern Adriatic from Trieste to Montenegro, each with a red box drawn around the area where the ensuing photos were taken. Many of them were from family holidays, so there were lots of pictures of the antics of Karlo's precocious daughter, and when the travel pictures were exhausted he showed me shots of some of his previous ships and then wound up with a video of me singing *Chiquitita* at the karaoke party.

I had not exactly forgotten to mention that I tried to sing *Chiquitita* at the karaoke party. . . but now I am embarrassed into it. Otherwise, from the evidence of the video, my description of the party is right-on, except that I failed to remember the Bosun's bear-hugging Karlo from behind and bouncing him around the floor, which looked like quite a feat since Karlo is probably 15 kilos heavier. Karlo assured me that I had been "queen of the party, the only woman on board." Watching all these antics on the computer screen, I had another one of those "disconnect" moments, when my entire previous life seemed to bear no relation to present time.

The photos of the Balkan coast were marvelous – hundreds of islands floating in turquoise waters, craggy coastlines, stony ruins, venerable churches, ancient olive trees and a history that goes back to the Phoenicians. The New World looks awfully new by comparison. Not only did I arrive on board utterly ignorant of the history of the now-independent countries that made up the nation-state of Yugoslavia when it was invented after the First World War, but I had only the vaguest idea of where they are. When you meet seafaring people who have been all over the world, your relative ignorance becomes painfully obvious.

This morning I asked my shipmates what they loved about being at sea. Charles first mentioned the variety – "not the same house, not the same job, not the same bus" – and new ships and new places. He also said that he appreciated the opportunity to have longer conversations with people than would be the norm at home. I assume he also meant getting to know people you wouldn't normally meet at home. He said that when he was at sea he enjoyed the feeling of being cut off – isolated by the lack of communications with the rest of the world. And then he said "warm nights on the upper deck, with all the phosphorescence in the water. It's peaceful." Ian was a bit more prosaic: "I've always enjoyed the outdoors, and this" – pointing out the porthole –"certainly qualifies, if you exclude the big hunk of steel between you and it."

Like snowflakes, no two waves are alike.

Day Thirty-six, at Sea: The day opens a featureless gray, the sea choppy on top of a long undulating swell from the south. Whitecaps toss about without rhyme or reason. Solid squalls charge us every few minutes, and a look at the horizon produces half a dozen more, slatey smudges between sky and sea. All this makes for shakes and shudders and sudden lurches of the ship. I nominate another nautical term: *wobble.*

We met the new Filipino Second Officer on the Bridge yesterday. He was very polite and obviously nervous with three foreigners on his watch at the same time. He wanted to answer all questions within a degree of latitude, a minute of time, so he got flustered instead. The Captain would expect clear answers; we would be happy with approximations that didn't stress the Second so much. But such men are trained to be precise. They have to be. Even though he's more comfortable with the unpredictability of the sea, the Captain loves to give precise answers too. Yesterday it was, "We will arrive in Panama at 0100 twelfth August." This means he's got a date for the Canal for that day. Will they be sending us through in the morning or the afternoon? He is parsimonious with the details. He likes keeping us in suspense; it heightens the drama of our days.

How does one talk about self-loathing without sounding ridiculous? A lot of people probably feel it, but it's seldom shared. It happens to me whenever I see myself on film. This is surely a hand-me-down from my mother – I'm willing to bet she felt much the same way, and I'm also sure she went to lengths to make sure I wouldn't. But there's no escaping the legacy of abuse.

I think of her now, sitting over drinks listening to men talk. She always said men liked good listeners. But, you can lose track of who you are when you're focused on pleasing another person that way. Rather than

104

show off, you let the other person show off; you retire into the shadows and the other gets to feel he's impressing you. He's grateful.

There's "good listening" as a social skill that you use to make yourself more attractive, and there's good listening-really-listening, which hears under the skin of the other to the heart. Too often the one gets in the way of the other. You listen self-consciously, always aware of the illusion you are projecting, always judging, always probing for the weaknesses behind the mask. Good-listening-really-listening lets all that go.

I'm pretty sure Mom didn't know the difference between these kinds of listening. She was just bent on feeling herself to be more attractive, and listening to men talk over drinks was easy for her. The problem was she didn't know when to stop drinking.

I think I am learning to tell the difference, for which I'm grateful, but my discernment is never a sure thing. I fell into a trap with Karlo, obsessing over whether he found me attractive, worrying about my body – is it too old? – wondering what it would be like to be touched again. This is painful to write because I am embarrassed by my seemingly endless capacity for obsessive thinking.

I am thinking also about betrayals, not only Mom's betrayals of Dad, but his of her. It was her dream to escape the abuse she grew up with, but she didn't know how to do it and instead married another abusee, someone who was often cruel to her, unyielding, hard. I really believe her drinking was a response to that; at least that's the narrative I've held to ever since we went to France together in 1992. She could never talk about it.

How does this relate to now? To me here on this ship in the middle of the incredible ocean? I have had thoughts of suicide, which I suspect were no stranger to Mom either. Those are the times I just don't see a way clear to making things any better, when the pain has me in its grip, when I'm not sleeping well, when Roger is being ornery and I can't even drag myself into the kitchen to cook. At home I have resources. I get up and walk down to the gate. I pet the dogs. I let cat Tricksy snuggle under my shirt and try to feel the love she's purring. I breathe. These things often get me through. Out here, I have only my tricky mind for company. I dreamt about Tricksy the other morning. She was in "merge mode," burying her nose into the hollow of my throat, her warm body flattened out against mine. I needed that. And then suddenly I had the fear that she wouldn't be there when I got home, that something terrible had happened to her, and that this dream was her signing off. Fear is the opposite of love. In my case, I can't have love without the fear of losing it. Losing it, then, realizes my worst fear . . . that I am not loved.

I half-suspect that Roger knows that this flirtation with Karlo was something I was looking for, an affirmation of some part of me that he must be conscious he's ignoring. The irony for me is that, as fun as it's been, it turns out to be an affirmation of what I don't want. One of these days, I will indeed weep.

Back in the port of Sydney, the jitney driver and I were talking about the weather. I said to him I had just come from the tropics and I wasn't used to Sydney temperatures, and he said he had just booked a holiday for himself and "the wife" at a resort in Fiji. I didn't comment on Fiji except to say, "It was nice and warm there."

"Yeah," he went on, "it's a kind of reconnection holiday for us."

"How nice," I said.

Meanwhile, of course, I have to accept that all my hurt and anger at not hearing from Roger in those first few weeks were just wasted energy. Poof. Will this new understanding help me to be any less obsessive?

Today is Slop Chest Day. I was just lying down to listen to Berlioz' *Symphonie Fantastique* when the phone rang. "Hello Sandra! This is Bosun."

"Hi Bosun, how are you?"

"I fine, how are you?"

"Very fine, thank you."

"Sandra, I want to ask favor from you, that you won't tell the Captain."

"Maybe," I said, "Depends what it is."

"We know you can buy bottle of Jack Daniels, the crew want you to buy bottle and give us and don't tell Captain."

It didn't take me long to think. "No, I don't think I can do that, Bosun. When Cristi, Lila and I wanted to do something nice for the crew, we asked the Captain about buying beer for you, but he said he controls all liquor aboard the ship, so he suggested chocolates instead. I know he feels strongly about that and I don't want to violate his trust. I still have almost two weeks left on board, and what would happen if he found out?"

"Okay, I understand."

"I'm sorry, Bosun."

"Okay, thank you."

At least for a while, I was a big hit with the crew!

106

Day 37, at Sea: I vowed I would stay off the computer today – the vertebrae between my neck and back are so strained that all the muscles in that part of me are frozen solid – so most of the day has been spent lying down flat, not even reading or listening to music. It's painful to move my head in conversation at meals. Painful to sit in a chair on deck. Painful to look in any direction whatever. And today this discomfort has set off the fibromyalgia alarm and the whole body hurts.

But I have to write about the little surprise I was given today.

Last night at dinner Manny handed me a small folded-up oblong of paper that I took to be a receipt from the Slop Chest, so I just tucked it away in my crossword puzzle book to look at later. In the lounge after dinner, I opened it and was not a little alarmed to read:

> Sandra,
> Tomorrow, Sunday at 10:20 AM please come to the bridge but be alone.
> Best regards,
> See you tomorrow.

The only two people likely to be on the Bridge in the morning are the Officer of the Watch – Third Mate Denny – and the Captain. Somehow, I felt the note had been from the latter, but I couldn't be sure. Why hadn't he signed it? And that specific time – 10:20 – what could be happening at exactly 10:20? Had I done something so irretrievably culturally insensitive that I was about to be court marshaled? Keelhauled?

I hesitated to show it to anyone, but finally decided to ask Karlo what he thought of it. He opened it, read it, mused a moment and said, "Ah, no signature. . . . maybe you will have a pleasant surprise. Ah . . . I will come there. I'm sure it will be all right." This was marginally comforting, and I went to bed swearing I would not let my imagination carry me away.

Lying flat on the bed for most of the morning, I watched the time tick by, every hour putting ice on my neck for five minutes. At 10:15 I was just getting ready to go up to the Bridge when Denny knocked on my door: "The Captain wants to see you." With some trepidation I mounted the two flights of stairs and opened the door. Silhouetted in the light from the forward windows stood the imposing figure of the Captain, hands clasped in front of him and wearing full captain's regalia and a big grin. Karlo was off to my right snapping a photo of my surprised reaction; he, too, was in dress blues. It was wonderful: blue jackets and trousers, gold stripes, brass buttons, blue ties, black shoes, *socks,* and Karlo even had his white cap under his arm. It was immediately obvious they were putting on this little show for my benefit, because he quickly handed the camera to Denny and joined the Captain and me for the obligatory photos. I had said to Karlo a couple of weeks ago that it would be nice to see them in uniform, since all the Captain has been able to muster so far (in Papeete, I think) was a white short-sleeved shirt with epaulettes and long pants. We clowned around for the camera and I admired all the details – the buttons, the stripes – while they explained their insignia, and Denny brewed some coffee. We had a delightful visit for twenty minutes before they both had to go change clothes for cabin inspection, for which they were not about to risk either the amazement or amusement the crew by going room to room in uniform. Before leaving the Bridge, the Captain said, "So, you are sure you don't want to stay on board? We go to Philadelphia, then Rotterdam. Panama will always be there."

It would be hard not to feel real affection for these guys.

Day Thirty-eight, at Sea: We've lost that deep roll from the south and are now battering our way into a headwind off our starboard bow in choppy seas, puffy clouds skidding and colliding over cobalt blue water capped with foam. The spume blows away from the crests of the waves in smoky rainbows. Under the fleeting shadows of the clouds the sea dulls and seems to flatten out as if someone had spread it with ashes. About every tenth bow wave is big enough to send spray up over the containers on the foredeck.

Now, allow me to introduce the new nautical term *wiggle.* The ship's motion is short and choppy, like the seas, and the *Louise* is behaving just like a fat lady trying to squeeze her bottom into an upholstered chair.

Email to: Roger, by way of the Captain's email
Subject: Arrival in Panama
Hello, love,
Just to let you know that all is well. Crossing Tropic of Capricorn today on a straight ENE course to Panama. We're scheduled for the Canal on August 12th, arriving in Manzanillo late in the day.
Since the hour for tying up to the dock is always a little uncertain, and the ship has immigration things to do before anyone can disembark, perhaps it would be better for me to just take a taxi to wherever you're going to be.

108

I'll send you another note when we're closer to Panama to confirm arrival time, so check your mail when you're on the road. You can also check with the port agent in Colón.
Please reply to this mail so that I know you have received it and to let me know where you'll be and send me the phone number in case I have to try to reach you from the port. Looking forward to seeing you!
Love,
S

The punch line to the uniform story is that Karlo wrote the note.

Day Thirty-nine, at Sea: The ride is getting bumpier. Charles and Ian said they had trouble sleeping last night – I rocked like a baby. But this morning there was absolutely no way to stand still enough to do a sun salutation. I could barely stay on my feet. So I did all the floor poses and then trotted on down to the gym to push a little harder on the bicycle. I've skipped the past two days because of my neck, but the frequent icing and the rest have made it better. We're hitting squall after squall, and every once in a while the bow slaps into a wave with such force that it resounds through the hull and feels as if we've crashed into something solid. I'm weaving back and forth in my chair as I write.

Both Lila and Cristi were wearing small black elastic wrist bands when we left Panama. Each band has a white plastic button that is supposed to be positioned exactly over an acupressure point three fingers up the inner arm from one's wrist between the flexor tendons. Lila tended to be a lot queasier than Cristi, and she was wearing them in what I considered almost calm seas. Cristi said they had saved her in that storm in the North Atlantic, however. Lila had the kind thought to donate hers to me as she left the ship, in case we should run into any of the Captain's predicted bad weather. Today I'm wearing them. I honestly don't know if they're helping or not, but I did feel my stomach wasn't exactly in the right place during yoga, so I thought I'd give them a try. Beats pills.

I suppose even the most congenial people can become tiresome after a while at close quarters. Charles turns out to be a heavy teaser, and with Ian he exploits the historic rivalry between the states of Victoria and South Australia *ad nauseam*. With me, he makes cynical remarks about "hubby" and cracks off-color jokes. Maybe he finds my being alone suggestive of some moral laxity. I suppose that, after thirty years as a clergyman, he's more than familiar with all forms of human frailty, but I don't find his raillery amusing.

Poor Ian, meanwhile, has a nasty cold that has settled in his chest. They've both had colds, but Charles's has been much lighter. Still, for days the two of them have been hauling their handkerchiefs out of their pockets and honking and hacking over our lunches and dinners in ways that make me want to scurry out of the Mess for fear of contagion. I'm taking precautions!

I went up to the Bridge to look at the charts and ask about the weather. Third Mate Denny explained that there's no specific weather system we're dealing with, then he showed me on the chart all the wavy lines of the currents, each with a little arrow at one end pointing west-southwest – right on our starboard bow, which is also where the wind is. "We've got everything against us," Denny said. At our normal 86 engine revolutions, we're making only 18 knots. Our position is around the Tuamotou Archipelago (not visible to us, but there's a lot out here in the Pacific that isn't visible to us), about nine days out of Panama. He said we'd make up the time we're losing at this speed, however. While I was there, the Captain came up, and I felt the need to explain that I had just wanted to ask where the weather was coming from. He said, "Oh, you haven't seen anything yet. These waves are only about three meters. You wait."

I had despaired of ever getting Filipino food to eat. I guess nobody believed I would eat it, so Cook has been going to the trouble of cooking fish for me almost every day, and sometimes twice. This always comes with the standard potatoes and buttered vegetable, however. Last night the menu said sausage and sauerkraut, which he knew I wouldn't eat, so he put a couple of vegetarian spring rolls on the table instead. Just as Manny was telling me what they were, Charles spotted the plate and tried to co-opt it for himself (he did this once with the morning grapefruit too – I think he just isn't thinking that some of the food on the table is served family-style). Knowing the spring rolls were going to be my only dinner, I snatched the plate away from him and said, "I think these were intended to share, Charles." I generously gave him one, and then I asked Manny if there was any of Cook's "sweet and sour" sauce in the Galley. There wasn't, but Manny mixed up a fair approximation himself that he calls "vinegar onion sauce." It had a nice bite to it – sambal. I asked him to keep it in the fridge for me and today I had the sense to ask for rice with my chicken instead of potatoes and then I liberally sprinkled the sauce over everything. We're getting there!

Ian is feeling better today, so I asked if he'd like a game of Ping-Pong (which he calls table tennis) after lunch. When he first came on board, he described how he had played almost every evening from Melbourne to Manzanillo with the Chief Engineer on one of the *Louise's* sister ships. He was game to play today, but I will need a lot of practice before I'm able to offer him any competition. He's got a nice back-hand slider serve that I am challenged to return. He graciously agreed to volley back and forth with me until I improve.

Day Forty, at Sea:
Email to: Alison, Helen
Hello dears,
I've just found out that the reason I can't communicate with Roger may be that Yahoo doesn't contract for our particular satellite service, and of course out here in the ocean that is all we've got. Meanwhile at home, our houseguests all have Yahoo too. I know I've been able to communicate with Alison, because she has responded to the ship, but I also know she's leaving for Holland shortly and won't be able to serve as a relay to Roger after she's gone. (Al, tell me your departure date.) So, Helen, if you get this, please reply – this is the Captain's email address – I need to know if I can relay messages through you to Roger about my arrival time. He can't send mail to me either, so he'll have to send it to you with a request that you forward it. I hope this isn't too much of an imposition. Meanwhile, please forward him this message. Thanks, and kisses! Only eight days away from Panama.
Love, S

It is also probable that Costa Rica's monopoly telecommunications company hasn't contracted for our satellite service either, since I haven't been able to reach Roger by the sat-phone. I asked the Captain what the Company's port agents based in other countries like mine do? They have their own modems and can link to the satellite directly. Costa Rica is not the only backward country in the world – the Philippines has better service! – but I bet their number is diminishing rapidly. All my fellow passengers – from Switzerland, U.S. and Australia – have cell phones that work all over the world. We can't even take ours across the border into Panama. This is worth a letter to the editor.

You can smell the tropics. Out on deck in the dark, the stars faintly winking on and off as low clouds stream invisibly across the sky, there's a new, heavy warmth to the air. I feel it on my skin, taste it in my nose; it's humid, soft and kind. Maybe this is what they mean by "balmy tropical nights." It feels like home.

Yesterday I was again feeling the press of time. Not enough time left, not enough time to do what I set out to do, what am I going to do if I don't get it done? Nine days to Manzanillo yesterday. Eight today. Tomorrow only a week. It's getting harder to remember even the details of the ports we've visited. All is receding, dissolving in the wake of the Louise as she plods faithfully onward, now only three hours west of Costa Rica time.

This voyage has been a dream. Reality got suspended for a while as I headed off into the day before. But it's still there where I'm going to, and what will have changed? Anything? Will I have changed? Some things have become a little clearer on the far horizon. Instead of reflections in layers of vapor, I can see some solid objects now. I will try to understand these better in the coming days. It makes me sad to leave the ship, but I have another life that I have to find again.

After the Captain sent my emails announcing our arrival on the 12th, he now tells me it's been put back to the 13th and I feel a small reprieve. There may be another barbecue party before I go, although the Captain doesn't yet know where. The poop, like the bow, is awash. He said we would have this weather for at least four more days. This morning there was a bit of a lee up on F Deck, so I grabbed my folding chair and climbed up there in the sun. The railings were encrusted with salt. I perched my feet on the lowest rail and turned my face skyward. I noticed that the sun is tracing a higher arc in the heavens these days, and I could feel salt spray on my toes.

Day Forty-one, at Sea: The planet Venus is so bright that she casts her pale glow across the surface of the sea just like her bigger sister the Moon.

I can see how this last passage could get long. Since both my shipmates are seasoned sea travelers, they display little curiosity about the ship, so, unlike with Lila and Cristi, the workings of the *Louise* are not a daily subject of conversation. In fact, conversation frequently flags. Weather. Sports. Shore arrangements on arrival in Tilbury. Travel in general. Very few personal questions, although Charles did ask me last night why I had moved to Puerto Rico. I suspect Aussies of being reserved in similar ways to their Canadian cousins. Lila was much more "American" in the sense of talking candidly about her life and her family and her stresses, her job, her pension, her plans. So she invited more personal confidences. Cristi was more reserved, but she was very good at asking the kinds of questions that stimulate conversation. With these two men, however, I frequently find myself less and less curious about them and their lives. They're probably feeling the same way about me. Whatever, there is almost nothing to draw us together outside of mealtimes. I told them both this morning at breakfast about the stars last night, and how bright Venus was, but all either of them said was "Mmmm." So the natural world doesn't interest them. The engine room doesn't interest them. Costa Rica doesn't interest them. I've led the way up to the Bridge a couple of times, but they seem to have no questions beyond what the weather is going to do. They've been on ships before. Perhaps it's also true that women *always* have something in common, so it's easier to find things to talk about with relative strangers. And it occurs to me that people who travel widely – professional travelers, if you like – may prefer *not* to get too close to people they are not likely to meet again. Their civility and amiability would always be general, not specific.

The social dynamic on board has also changed because the Captain is on a diet. One of the first times he joined us in the lounge before dinner, he was drinking a coke. He's allergic to alcohol, so naturally we all joked about his being the "designated driver." But he had also quit smoking. We swapped quitting-smoking stories for a few minutes, and he said he had gained 14 kilos. I looked down at his soft drink, and the words just popped out of my mouth, "So now you are addicted to sugar." I don't know what on earth motivated me to say that, but he gave me a penetrating look and said, "You're right."

A couple of days later, he came into the lounge obviously stressed, and he started eating chocolates, peeling the foil off them one by one and stuffing them into his mouth right on top of each other. It was painful to watch. Silently, I moved the bowl of mixed nuts in front of him and slid the chocolates away. "Thank you," he said.

"I just hate to see you eating candy like that," I said.

We then began to notice his consumption of ice cream. No matter what was on the menu for dessert, the Captain had a big bowl of chocolate-chip ice cream. I mean Big. Piled high. There were meals when all he had was ice cream. Once or twice, we observed Manny taking a bowl of ice cream up to the Bridge or the E Deck conference room.

When we were in Sydney, the Captain wanted to stop for ice cream at 11:40 in the morning. I don't know why I felt the need to act like his mother, but I said, "Wait till after lunch." So he bought some cashews, and he ended up not having any ice cream at all.

I guess it was shortly after Sydney that he failed to show up in the Mess for dinner. And he didn't show up in the lounge either. The officers don't appear at breakfast, so it wasn't until lunch the next day that I was able to say, "We missed you yesterday evening, Captain."

"I am on a diet. No more dinner. No more sweets." And then he added, *"Soy hombre de palabra."* I am a man of my word. (He speaks creditable Spanish, but he rarely says anything to me in that language.)

The result has been that we see less of the Captain than formerly, and my new shipmates have seen him hardly at all. He strides into the Mess at lunch, booming, "Good afternoon, good appetite," sits down, immediately begins speaking to his fellow officers in his native tongue and rarely, if ever, directs a comment or question to our table. I think Charles and Ian find this a bit chilling, from a social point of view, because it seems to intensify the general lack of volubility in our small circle.

A couple of nights ago, the Captain did show up at dinner and ate some cereal, and then he joined Chief Engineer in the lounge afterwards. As I passed the door on my way out, I said, "It's good to see you this evening, Captain," and they both invited me to join them. He was in high spirits and told one funny story after another, keeping Karlo and me doubled over with laughter for a couple of hours. Maybe the three of us have arrived at a level of comfort with each other that might be felt as a little exclusive by the others; I don't know. Certainly the day in Sydney set a new tone for us. But it's also true that the Captain was much more inclined to tell stories when Cristi and Lila were on board. Perhaps it has something to do with being charming to women. Whatever, between stories the other night I said to him, "All you need is an audience," and he gave me another of his penetrating looks and said, "You're right."

Who knows what effect we have on other people? We meet, we know each other only briefly, we connect in our limited ways, and then we part. The Captain has lost five kilos. He did indeed look slimmer in his uniform, and he's obviously pleased with himself. I'm glad.

Day Forty-two, at Sea: This is the first day we've seen a perfectly cloudless sky. Normally, even on the sunniest days, there are clouds piled up on the horizon, so that, even though you're moving through space, the clouds give you the sense that there is a limiting circle around you, that the whole circle of ocean within the horizon is itself moving. Today, to the east the sea has a metallic sheen, almost white where it meets the sky. Elsewhere along the horizon, it is just a clear knife-edge of deep, infinite blue.

We still have our headwind, but this is the first day in four that the winds have been less than 20 knots, and the ship has settled back into a slow, rock-a-bye-baby roll, very conducive to sleep. I slept in this morning. After hunkering down on a barstool for a couple of hours last night listening to the Chief Engineer's stories, I realized that my upper back and neck simply won't tolerate sitting in that position so long; I had to take a heavy pain pill when I went to bed and so was too groggy to make it to breakfast. At nine, I made myself a cup of instant coffee in the lounge and ate a stale granola bar. Waiting for the water to heat up, I found myself staring at the rubber plant tied down to the shelf in front of one of the portholes, and it suddenly occurred to me that, out here in the endless blue ocean, I am beginning to miss the color *green*.

Email to: Five friends based in the U.S.
Subject: Arrival in Panama
Hello everyone, I need your help. I am unable to reach Roger – or, it seems, anyone in Costa Rica – from the ship to tell him when I am arriving. Could anyone or everyone who gets this message please forward it to him so he has the details of my arrival? Then please reply to this address – the Captain's email – so that I know it's gone through. Thank you so much! Looking forward to being home.
Love,
S

Listening to their talk for so many weeks, I am getting a decidedly unromantic view of the life of a seaman. A typical contract for a senior officer is four months on, two off. Chief Engineer Karlo is on "permanent" contract, so this is the schedule he lives with. Except that there's a clause in the contract that says the Company can extend you, and this is what happened to Karlo, for two additional months. He was supposed to sign off in Savannah at the end of September, and now it's Rotterdam at the end of November. Ship assignments are unpredictable, so you can be flown anywhere in the world to sign on to your new ship – Hong Kong, Aukland, Marseilles, anywhere – and almost always on short notice. Your bags have to be packed and standing by the door.

Shipping companies normally work with crewing agencies to supply the personnel on board; in Karlo's case the shipping company owns the crewing agency. English is the language of international shipping, and to reinforce this policy the Company likes to mix up crews of various nationalities, although this doesn't always work. Once Karlo's captain was Polish and didn't bother to take meals in the Mess and his Asian officers preferred to eat with the crew, so Karlo ate all his meals alone for four months. It's hard to imagine living with virtually no social contact for four whole months. He said that in all that time, aside from phone calls, he probably spent an aggregate of one hour with his captain.

Manny, the Messman/Steward, the lowliest of the low, works nine months in order to get a month off with his family. He is the only one on board who serves at meals and cleans the cabins, so he's working seven days a week. There is also just a single cook preparing meals for 22 people, all day, every day. Overtime pay is limited to 160 hours a month. Right now, the ship is running four crew members short, which means everybody works more but isn't getting compensated for all the extra time. Senior officers aren't eligible for overtime. Money is the name of the game.

One of the lessons I seem to be learning is that the idea of this trip was the fantasy of my aging, death-defying self. The idea of a long freighter voyage appealed to my sense of daring, and even though I knew it was born of desperation it made me feel braver, younger. I got plenty of reinforcement of this from friends. One even said, "You are my hero!" For a while, I could imagine myself to be other than a middle-aged woman with too many physical ailments; I could pretend I was someone else. This is what I have been doing on board. It has been a much more social trip than I imagined, and I have immensely enjoyed living outside my usual self.

My body reminds me, however. It insists. It just won't be ignored, and this is something I am going to have to learn to accept.

In spite of this disjunction between my real and my fantasy selves, I have had many moments of pure contentment on this ship, at sea. At sundown today, for instance, I look out at the horizon and see a flotilla of puffy pink clouds trailing gray wakes in formation off our starboard bow, herding us home. I am moved to smile at all the fuss I create for myself. Indeed, I feel a moment of peace.

Day Forty-three, at Sea: There was quite a to-do yesterday when the Captain told Charles at lunch that he would have to come up with his medical certificate or disembark in Panama. This was about as brusque a delivery as he could have offered; in fact, Charles felt it as "aggressive." I know the Captain well enough to know that the pressures of business make him irritable, and in this case I suspect he was even feeling a little defensive. Charles had not been informed by his travel agent that he would need original documents, or even copies, for the ship's captain, although he happened to have most of them. When he came on board, he told the Captain that he had sent the original certificate to the agent, who presumably had sent it on to the Head Office, so the Captain agreed to allow him to stay on board, pending confirmation from the Company. But the Head Office never responded to his email. Now, getting documents ready for the Immigration officials in Panama, he reminded the Company of the missing medical certificate and they can't find it. Bureaucrats. So the burden falls on the Captain to get Charles to come up with another one. In making this announcement, he was not helpful, but both Ian and I quickly suggested a number of ways for getting the document into the right hands on time, and the Captain agreed to make his email available. Charles is not especially computer-savvy, so in the afternoon I typed up a couple of email messages for him and saved them to a flash drive to take up to the Captain's office so that he could send them.

This really put a chill on things for Charles, however. Before dinner in the lounge, the Captain joined us. I think he was feeling a little sorry about the whole thing, and his tone was more sympathetic, but it was all Charles could do to respond civilly. He's deciding that he doesn't like this voyage much, and of course that affects the mood for the rest of us. For me, the episode was a reminder of the degree to which we human beings take things personally. Charles felt the Captain was being "aggressive," meaning toward him, and the Captain was feeling a bit defensive because he had let Charles board in the first place and now he was getting heat from the Head Office. In neither case was it necessary to feel under personal attack; it was just a typical bureaucratic tangle. But the reactions of both men have made it worse.

Last night I did not join the guys in the lounge after dinner, and my neck feels better. Let's see if I can keep it that way!

On the Bridge today, I handed in to Denny my evaluation form, having marked 100 points on all aspects of the ship's service. It occurred to me to say something about the food, but then I thought about Ernesto and all his efforts to give me an alternate whenever he was serving beef or lamb. And his soups have been so good! Then it occurred to me to say something about the broken exercise bicycle – the tension still can't be adjusted – but I didn't want to make any difficulty for the engineering crew. Finally, it occurred to me to mention the Serbo-Croatian at meals but, truly, I have no complaints about the Captain and I wouldn't want to make any difficulties for him. To me he has been kind, generous and informative – even if I have at times felt a little intimidated by him.

He came up to the Bridge while I was chatting with Denny, and he took the trouble to explain the physical forces that can break a ship, drawing pictures and even folding up a rough paper model to demonstrate. Waves in the Pacific have a longer frequency – distance between crests – than in the Atlantic, which presumably makes for more pacific passages. In serious weather, however, the amplitude, or height, of the waves can be equally dangerous. When a ship is evenly perched on top of a wave, exactly perpendicular to the crest, her own weight exerts tremendous pressures fore and aft, and she can snap in two. If she is exactly perpendicular to a trough, with nothing under her keel, stern and bow can snap in reverse. And you can't always run away from waves, or point the helm at an angle that would ease their battering. There might be shoals or other dangers to avoid on either side. "Water is the strongest thing in the world," the Captain said. He showed me how the longer the hull, the greater the danger of a ship's breaking up; and he stressed the importance of weight distribution in the loading of the cargo. The balance of forces within a ship – the weight of the cargo, fuel, ballast, as well as the materials that she's made of – can work to stabilize her in the face of extreme wind and waves. Tankers no longer run with empty hulls after discharging their load; they fill their holds with seawater. Still, the "graveyard of the supertankers" is around the Cape of Good Hope. And what of all these super container ships they're building?

I had been hoping to be able to stay up on the Bridge a while today – the atmosphere is quiet, the view spectacular – and to my happy surprise Denny served us coffee, and the Captain and I drank it, talking companionably for half an hour. He said the Company had offered him the command of one of its new super freighters and he had asked them what incentive there would be if he accepted. "You'll be Master of a new ship," they said. He'd captained a new ship once before, so new, in fact, that the super structure hadn't been finished yet. When finally at sea on her shakedown cruise, there were hundreds of things that needed fixing, including leaks in the hull. "Been there, done that," he told them. If there was no extra money in the offer, he was content to come back to the *Louise*, a ship he knows well. Seamen like to change ships, just to keep things interesting. But there's also a comfort in knowing all of a ship's little foibles and bad habits before you sail. There will always be surprises in any case.

As I was putting away my coffee cup in preparation to go below, the Captain recommended the passage from Panama to Kingston, Jamaica, Savannah, Philadelphia, Tilbury a few hours up the Thames, Rotterdam and back to Panama via Le Havre and New York for my next voyage. I would love it – I could briefly see a friend or two – and the six and a half hour sail up the Delaware past so many familiar landmarks would be a kind of homecoming. Denny asked me if I would voyage again, and I answered that I honestly didn't know. I mentioned some physical problems. I didn't mention the issue of money. But I looked out at that wide, bright ocean sparkling to the horizon all around us and thought that, yes, no matter the physical difficulties, if I could, I would do this again in a heartbeat. Just then the Captain – who complains that he doesn't even see the ocean anymore – cried out, "Look, tuna! Hundreds of them! Quick, Third, get your camera!" And we watched, each with a separate inner thrill for a few shared precious moments while the silvery tuna leapt straight up out of the sea all around us.

Dirty weather down south. Because of all the emailing for everybody, the Captain's been seeing my flash drive a lot lately, so he's been downloading to it colorful weather charts of the South Pacific that I share with my shipmates over afternoon tea. Just east of New Zealand a couple of days after we left, a low pressure system developed that would have been rough sailing through. Now that system has split up into three separate clockwise vortices, all lined up between New Zealand and Argentina, with 12-meter seas at the entrance to Cape Horn. He said there was no way this ship could go through all that, and we would have had to sit it out somewhere. He also said it was zero degrees Celsius in Melbourne yesterday. I'm glad we got out of there!

Finally an email from Roger. We'll meet up at the Four Points in Colón on the 13th. I'm looking forward to seeing him.

Day Forty-four, at Sea: A quiet day, with gloomy morning weather and sour moods, all of us waiting anxiously for some resolution to Charles's document problem, which we've been talking over *ad nauseam*. It turns out you get less sleep when you're chewing up time zones in reverse, which no doubt contributes to the general malaise. I spent most of the day immersed in another Conrad novel – what wonderful choices I made for reading material! When I get home I'll just have to plow through all the rest of him, he's that wonderful. Feeling a little guilty, I put in a couple of hours of editing time, and finally – just before dinner – the Captain was able to give us the news that Charles's travel agent had received his email and would send the medical certificate right away. A relief to all. Now Karlo seems to be coming down with Charles's cough and I'm beginning to feel I've been just a bit too long on board. For all their sea travel, neither Charles nor Ian has spent two weeks at sea with "nothing to look at." People are growing tired of each other, more irritable, more desirous of a change of subject, a change of scene. All this will happen soon enough; in only four days we'll have the Canal to entertain us. And in the interval I can start thinking about packing.

For most of the voyage, I have enjoyed being the first one in the lounge in the evenings, sipping my drink and watching the ocean and the play of light from closer range than I have on E Deck. Charles usually joins me in a few minutes, followed by Karlo, who always seems to be rushing to get there in time to fetch the ice for our drinks. I usually greet both Karlo and the Captain with some version of "How was your day?" or, "Hope there were no emergencies on the Bridge (or in the Engine Room)." Karlo always looks down at the ice tongs in his hand, shakes his head woefully and says, "Oh my God," then crosses the passage to the Galley with the ice bucket. The Captain, too, seems to enjoy appearing beleaguered, except his response is usually, "If you only knew." As comical as this is, I have to ask myself how often they get a little maternal or wifely sympathy at sea. This evening, after another martyred performance from Karlo, I turned to Charles and said, "Who's going to take care of these guys when I'm gone?"

Day Forty-five, at Sea: Thank God the elevator's been re-certified, because both my knees are shot. It was probably during the Ping-Pong game that I landed my right foot with force just as the deck was twisting under me in one of the Louise's yaws. And now the other knee is showing signs of weakness when I try to get out of a chair. No more gym, which means no more aerobic exercise till I get home, which means I'll lose half the conditioning I built up while on board. Still doing yoga, at least that part of my routine that's possible with the movements of the ship. It may be that just the constant need for sea-legs, the use of muscles in different ways, the stresses on joints when the floor turns away from you unexpectedly have all added up. It's becoming apparent to me that, if I do this again, I'll have to get some replacement parts first.

At night, the Bridge wants all of us in the forward cabins to tightly close our curtains. Stray light from the ship can interfere with the vision of the officer on watch; the Bridge itself is kept dark, with only the lights from the instruments and displays, and heavy curtains are drawn in front of the chart table. If anybody is out there on the wide ocean wandering around, you want to be able to see him. But after I turn off my reading light, I pull the curtains back again. From my pillow, I can look up and see the stars, big as ice cream cones in the vast uncovered sky. Being able to see them gives me moments of sweet calm whenever I wake during the night.

I've been thinking a lot about our old friend George, now gone, who at the age of 50 left his family of 13 children and went off alone on a small sailboat many years ago. One of his longer passages was in the Pacific, and he told me that looking up at the stars gave him such a feeling of the immensity and power of the universe that he became convinced that mere human beings could never begin to imagine the divine. He was sure it was out there, but far beyond our limited understanding. We human beings have a tendency to want to define things, take them apart, analyze them, prove our guesses in ways that will persuade others. We want to have all the right answers. Like George, I look at the night sky and can feel perfectly comfortable with the idea that I don't have any answers. Awe and joy when I behold the magnificent are food enough for this spirit.

121

The ocean is almost flat, with only a soft undulating swell, even though we still have the headwind. That's not likely to drop off until we're closer to land. There is only intermittent sun – I crawl up to F Deck with my folding chair, but the sky quickly clouds over. When the sun slides out from behind the clouds, the sea gets all gold and glittery like a treasure chest.

It's flattering to have another man pay you kind little attentions, including telling you that he enjoys your company. Perhaps this time together is flattering for both Karlo and me. He gets my undivided attention for an hour or two. I get appreciative masculine company. How tempting it would be if I were younger! In marriage – at least in mine – while there are certainly acts of kindness and thoughtfulness, we're no longer on our best behavior, we're not pretending to be something we're not, and, considering all the hours in a day, we spend very little time together and almost none of it in real conversation. So, at the very least, this time with the Chief Engineer has reminded me of something that's important to retain in a marriage, and that is present attention, the ability to see and appreciate what is different in the other, fresh laughter, and the quality of tenderness.

It is probably a cliché of international travel that a woman traveling alone is looking for an affair, preferably with an officer of a ship. Fantasizing about an affair is nearer the mark in my case. If Karlo had ever once put his hand on my arm and said, "Come upstairs," I'm still not sure what I would have done. There have been times when I've laughed at myself and thought, "He's probably a panter," or any number of other unappetizing things. At other times I've allowed myself to yearn to be folded up in his (or someone's) arms, and I have to admit the fantasy felt good. But I've crossed a threshold, now that I realize how much I'm looking forward to seeing my husband; the spell is broken, and I have nothing to regret. I'm satisfied with this much. The power of the human imagination is infinite; our reality limited. Who I fell in love with on this journey, really, was someone who has always been inside me but has been ignored for too long – my unfettered, unafraid self. I don't want to forget her again. Indeed, after a long life, it would be far worse to say that, instead of not being loved enough, I hadn't loved enough.

While Manny was in my cabin cleaning this morning, Bosun passed by the open door and said good morning. He asked me how many days I had left on board – it's only four. In fact, we are now on Costa Rica time. I told him I would miss being on the ship, and he had the kindness to say the crew would miss me, "the last of Charley's Angels." That's what they were calling Lila, Cristi and me all along – from the 70's TV series recycled into the Third World. "We're certainly old enough to be the original Charley's Angels!" I said, and he laughed. I'm glad he's forgiven me about that bottle of whiskey.

The sea is as gray and flat as flagstones. I said to the Captain last evening, "How calm it is!"

"The calm before the storm," he muttered.

I had to laugh at him. "You have been predicting bad weather this whole voyage, and it couldn't have been more beautiful!"

He reminded me that we had had to go 400 miles out of our way to escape all that mess off New Zealand. "The waves there are 14 meters now," he shook his head. "No way."

I didn't point out that we are *here* and not *there*. If it requires any particular genius to avoid bad weather, then our Captain is surely an ace, and I'm grateful. Maybe all along he's just been trying to keep us interested?

Day Forty-six, at sea: I finally got around to asking the Captain how long it would take to stop the ship. He started to answer that it would depend on conditions, the speed, currents, weather, wind, and so on, and I interrupted to ask, "So if there were a man overboard, what would happen?" Did I fail to mention that the Captain has dimples? He puckered them up and looked at me the way he does when he's about to spring the punch line and said, "If conditions are really bad, we just say a moment of silence and go on."

Karlo has been telling cargo stories again. He said tramp steamers drift around out in the middle of the Mediterranean, for example, so they can be ready to hop into a nearby port if they get a call to take a cargo from one place to another. They can respond far faster than if they are anchored in a harbor somewhere, and the additional fuel cost is negligible. The idea is to be always on the move; shipping companies lose money on idle ships. But the accountants have figured out that warehousing also costs money.

Keeping items in inventory – from spare parts to toothpaste – costs more than it does to keep them moving around the planet. Using his fingers to indicate quotation marks, Karlo said, "All cargo is on wheels." He told the story about a cargo of industrial steel coils that one of his previous ships had loaded in Fukushima, Japan, for transit across the Pacific and through the Panama Canal, destination Philadelphia. A month or so later his ship was in the Great Lakes and, when it took on cargo in Detroit, they found the exact same steel coils (just with the numbers sloppily painted over) which they then took east, up through 19 locks in the St. Lawrence Seaway, across the Atlantic, through Gibraltar and the Med, down through Suez, the Red Sea and on into the Indian Ocean and up the Pacific coast to Pusan, South Korea. The coils had traveled from Philadelphia to Detroit by train, the only terrestrial segment of their complete circumnavigation of the globe.

Now, tell me that's cheaper than sending them directly from Japan to Korea or storing them in a warehouse somewhere. I don't get it. There is something suspiciously unsustainable about all this. The system seems to be self-justifying. We need more cargo moving around, so we build bigger ships that will consume more fuel (albeit more efficiently per unit of cargo moved) and that need a wider Panama Canal to go through, the energy required for the construction of which – earth movers, dredgers, cement, steel – is absolutely beyond imagining. Just for historical perspective, the amount of material removed in the initial digging of the Canal would fill enough flatcars to circle the globe four times.

And, back to the California Red – I keep coming back to that well-traveled grapefruit – maybe we need to reexamine our consumption patterns here. Are we eating California grapefruit *just because we can get it?*

I've always suspected that sometimes the Captain and Chief Engineer are pulling my leg when I ask a question – I certainly caught them at it with Lila, whose boating experience is less than mine. But they'd have a hard time getting away with this with Charles, after all his years of service on Australian destroyers. His questions are always good ones and they elicit straight answers. Except yesterday evening when the Chief was regaling us with tales of disasters in the engine room. "So how do you start the engine if there's no electricity?" Charles asked. Karlo gave him a cagey look over his trifocals and said, "First you find the highest place in engine room. There you hang a block. Then you run a long rope through this block and wrap other end around engine flywheel. At the short end of rope you attach an empty oil drum, and then you start filling it with water. . ." We all cracked up before he could finish. Imagine starting a 900-ton lawnmower!

Day Forty-seven, at Sea: Gray, gray, gray. We have lost our bright sunshine and multi-hued waves. The sky is featureless, the sea calm, both meeting in a dark smudge along the horizon. Yesterday I was able to eke out 15 minutes of sun on E Deck, but today it looks hopeless. I may still be able to go up to the bow with Denny, but it won't be as beautiful as last time. I'd like to sit there for a while, however, and just soak in the quiet.

Last evening, the Captain asked me if I would do a voyage like this again. I said I'd love to. Then he teased me and said, "Now I can tell you the news; we're not going to Panama, we're heading for the Straits of Magellan." I said that this trip has been very special for me, but what were the chances of my finding a similar set of circumstances or people on another voyage? Karlo answered, "It would be more, it would be less; it wouldn't be the same."

How tempting it is to think that we, ourselves, are special: that this voyage was somehow designed for me, to give me joy, to teach me lessons; that these 49 days – which haven't seemed so long at all – were carved out of universal time so that I could float around in the biggest ocean on the planet and interact with this unique group of people, assembled on this ship solely for my benefit.

I said, "You guys will miss me when I'm gone."

"Aw, we will cry," Karlo said.

We've passed the Equator, we've passed the Galápagos, we've passed our last time zone – we're now on Eastern Standard, or Panama, time – and the *Louise* continues to plod through the peaceful sea. This morning I asked Third Mate if I could go up to what they call the "monkey deck" above the Bridge, the last deck and highest point on the ship – not counting the crow's nest – where the antennas, radar, anemometer and magnetic compass are. The deck, painted white, just a little rusty, looks bright, even on a dull day. From here you can get an almost 360-degree view – the only impediment is the stack, rising perhaps another story upward, with its one large and six small funnels. Up here it's quiet, not as quiet as the bow because there's a rhythmic huffing coming from the funnels, but still peaceful, and you can sense the solitude there, on top of the ship, on top of

125

the world. I asked Denny what the birds are; eight of them were careening and swooping above the starboard bow, occasionally diving into the water for a fish. He couldn't name them, but he said they were from the Galápagos. As with so many other new things we have met with on this trip, I will have to look them up when I get home.

Last trip to the bow. Although I had really wanted to go there by myself, I invited my shipmates. I'm not sorry I did. Ian and I both climbed the ladder to the tiny observation platform and stood there quietly, each in his own thoughts, for half an hour. He said only one word – Magnificent" – which needed no response. Charles stayed behind, seated on one of the mushroom-shaped bollards; Denny sat on the opposite side of the deck, waiting in his own quiet space. The sky stretched like a gray curtain to the horizon. The birds soared all around us. It was obvious they'd been using the bow as a roosting place, and they were curious about these two strange figures standing still as statues in their borrowed home. Some of them swooped to within a meter or two. The wind was still off our starboard bow, but kindly. When I faced into it, it whooshed in my ears, but when I turned my head to the side the silence was unearthly. No other sign of life, just the ever-moving, luminous sea.

At dinner the Karlo plunked a flash drive next to my plate with copies of the karaoke party videos for me to download to my computer. After we all ate, I took it upstairs, copied the files, and went back down to the lounge to return it to him. Karlo was seated at the corner of the bar nearest the door, so I didn't immediately see Igor and the Captain, who were seated at the table behind him. My momentum carried me into the room and when I rounded the corner of the bar, I gasped, "Captain!" On the table in front of him was a large dish of chocolate ice cream.

Igor and Karlo both laughed. "You want to share?" Igor asked. The Captain drew his beefy, tattooed arms protectively around his dish and sheepishly grinned. "It's going to be a rough couple days' work ahead," he said, as if that were an excuse for breaking his *palabra* about his diet. There was nothing I could graciously do except smile and say, "Goodnight, gentlemen," and I went back upstairs, their laughter ringing in my wake.

Day Forty-eight, at Sea: We'll be anchoring in the approaches to the Canal around midnight, waiting for our entry and passage at first light. The only sign of life a lone freighter on the northern horizon; later in the day

126

there will be many more. At midday under a lowering sky the shadowy blue headland of the peninsula rises eerily off to port, draped in mist behind a curtain of rain. The Americas. How well I remember leaving this place!

I'm already half-packed, and there's not much more to write, except for the final chapter, which I will do at home.

This morning it was sunny on F Deck, so I hauled my folding chair up the ladder and parked there for a while. The sea ahead was like a million tiny suns and the breeze was heavy with moisture. For the last few days the crew has been taking advantage of the calm seas to paint number-two crane, using a complication of ropes and bosun's chairs to swing around in mid-air as they hammer off the rust, then prime and paint. This morning Bosun, in his yellow jumpsuit and safety harness, hailed me from his slender perch hanging aft of the crane. I signed to him that I was sunbathing and, laughing heartily, he signed back that I should take off all my clothes. Great jokers, these Filipinos. Could it have been he who called to invite me to the karaoke party?

Last night I spent a couple of hours with the Captain and Karlo, as they told their last round of stories. I won't see much of them tomorrow, but the Captain has given me permission to watch maneuvers between the Canal and the dock at Manzanillo, so I'll be able to say goodbye to him then before I pick my way down the accommodation ladder for the last time.

As I started to say goodnight, both Karlo and the Captain said, "Wait! You have to come up to F Deck." They wouldn't tell me what for – typical of their love of surprises. We all piled into the elevator and went up to Karlo's day room. There on the wall was the "upside down" map of the world, Australia at the top, Canada at the bottom. Lila had told me about this map – the one in her office at work used to give visitors a shock – but when I finally saw it last night on Karlo's wall, I couldn't believe how disorienting it was. I loved it. Quickly, he untacked it, folded it up and gave it to me. Both of them wanted me to have this parting present, and as I headed for the stairs Karlo said, "You won't forget us!" and the Captain called, "We'll remember how you tried to run away from us in Sydney!"

Back in my room, I laughed at myself. All this time I had been living in a fairy tale that had a happy ending. I got what I wanted.

127

Day Forty-nine, Panama Canal: According to Karlo, we were getting a jump on the Canal by going through at night, picking up the pilot in the bay at 10:45 and heading straight for the first Miraflores lock. I said I thought that only small ships were allowed through at night, and he reminded me that this *is* a small ship. With less than a meter's canal clearance on either side of the hull, this is a small ship? It seemed that once again the Company had done some pushing to get us through early to try make up for our day of lost time. As one of the largest shipping companies in the world, it must wield some clout. Ian and I agreed we would get up to watch our passage through Miraflores, and Charles said he was going to bed as usual.

A little past midnight, something woke me and I quickly dressed and went outside, just in time to see the pilot boat chug up alongside. Back to bed. Up at 2:15 to find Ian on deck where we snacked on a couple of granola bars and took a few pictures while we watched our passage through the two miter gates of the lock. Outside the foggy circle created by the lights, all was dark, humid and close. The visitor center was a blackened hulk. It seemed there were fewer hardhats around. I sat against the bulkhead on F Deck until I realized that the *Puente Centenario* was not lighted except for street lights – how magnificent it would look with those great wings illuminated against the sky! And so back to bed, to awaken in time for breakfast and to find the ship making a slow progress through Gatún Lake.

And now the *Louise*, along with four other freighters, is anchored in the lake while other ships come chugging through ahead of us, waiting for what? What clout?

We were parked within sight of the Gatún Locks for five hours, and the time seemed long indeed as I thought about Roger driving that day from David, up near the Panamanian border, to Colón, there to wait for me to take a taxi to the hotel. Finally at 2:00, the propeller ground to life again and we were on our way, the last leg of my journey. Charles and I stood on the starboard side of E Deck to watch our passage through the first of the three chambers. It was his first Canal transit, so it must have been for him that the tug boats tooted as they peeled away from the hull just in time to escape being crunched between the *Louise* and the lock wall. The lead tug was the *Los Santos,* surely a good omen! After what seemed like a precipitous drop of nine meters, and before the *Louise* started to labor into the second chamber, I returned to my cabin – I've seen it before, I thought jadedly. Then something moved me, a strange little "what if?", and I went back out on deck in spite of the total improbability that Roger would be there. Suddenly I heard an unfamiliar voice hailing me through a megaphone, and I saw my husband on the observation platform, not three meters away from the *Louise*'s D Deck, surrounded by a whole crowd of French tourists waving excitedly, their guide continuing to holler my name, and all apparently delighted that my husband and I were to be reunited at last. I waved and threw kisses while Roger saved the moment with his mobile phone camera.

Later I learned that the ship originally had been scheduled for the western lane, but through the intervention of the Canal authorities – even they are suckers for the romantic moment – the *Louise* shifted at the last minute into the eastern lane, closer to the tourist observation platform. I had seen her bow slice suddenly to starboard just as we were entering the locks, but I thought perhaps there had been a miscommunication with the pilot. This little maneuver explains how the Captain could assure me later that there would be a "taxi" waiting for me at the security gate.

There's not much left of the journey to tell, except that now I was really ready to disembark. But, of course, there was some hold-up, and after passing Manzanillo – its giant blue gantries shrinking into the distance behind us – we headed five miles out to sea to drift around for a while. Fortunately, I was prepared by our previous dockings for this kind of delay, so I didn't work myself into a fret at how much time it was taking. I got into my shore clothes, snapped my suitcases shut and read the introduction to Trollope's *The Eustace Diamonds,* a book I had found in the lounge and had no plans to take with me. I had left my door open and Igor looked in, still in his gray jumpsuit, surveyed my latched suitcases and asked, "Contract finish?" He had been positively verbose in these last few days!

Around 5:30, I went down to the Officers' Lounge and poured my last drink on board. Within a minute or two, I could feel our massive rudder move, and the *Louise* started her final beeline into the port while I stood in the window and watched all the freighters at anchor sliding past us with increasing speed. Ten minutes later the phone rang. It was First Mate Enrique inviting me up to the Bridge to watch maneuvers. How good of the Captain to remember!

On the Bridge I kept on the port side well out of everyone's way. The Captain, still in his sunglasses, was standing behind his massive control panel, there was an able seaman at the helm, and First Mate stood between me and the Captain, ready for any orders. The first order was, "First Mate, open torpedo tube number one." Always the joker.

Within a few minutes, the pilot strode onto the Bridge, obviously a little taken aback to find me sitting there. He and the Captain communicated almost solely in Spanish; I guessed the pilot assumed I wasn't conversant in the language. One of the first things the Captain said to him was, "She is heavy loaded and doesn't stop so fast." Very quickly the pilot started calling out headings in English, and the Captain repeated them to the man at the helm. This, of all the ports we had entered, was surely the trickiest. As we approached the gap in the breakwater – it couldn't be wide enough for our ship! – the pilot called out, "Hard to port!" and I could feel the ship groan into her turn even as the rocks were slipping past us on either side. A second "hard to port," then a series of three "hard to starboards" as the *Louise* wound her way through a very sinuous channel. Finally the order came: "Left full rudder!" and I watched fascinated as we pivoted 180 degrees on our bow and, with a tug nosing her stern, the *Louise* slid aft-end-first into a berth just a few meters behind another container ship with a fuel barge rafted alongside. Both the Captain and the pilot were out on the starboard wing as the linesmen called out the shrinking meters between the hull and the dock over their walkie-talkies, just like calling out depth soundings in a fog. It was a flawless parallel parking job.

During maneuvers, I went briefly outside on the port wing. The sun had set behind the *cordillera*. The sky deepened and sighed out into that pellucid clarity it has in the tropics during those few moments before the stars come out, and the lights of the ships at anchor sparkled in the opalescent sea. I stood with my hands on the rail, breathing it in and feeling a kind of peaceful glory at how beautiful it was, at how beautiful I felt being a part of that moment, at how wonderful – full of wonder – the whole voyage had been.

Manzanillo. This is where I came in.

130

Epilogue
Panama to Costa Rica
The Quality of a Destination

The story wouldn't be complete without an account of what happened to Roger and our car after I left. Only because I was the one to pick it up from the dealer, our car is in my name only. We've never bothered to change this, since it never presented a problem in Costa Rica and it would have involved paying sales taxes all over again. And it never occurred to us that the Panamanian government wouldn't allow the car out of the country without me in it!

Following the instructions of friends familiar with the border crossing, we had gone to the National Registry in Costa Rica to get an exit permit for the car, but it turned out to be good for only 30 days. In order to enable Roger to go back to Panama to pick me up two months later, we got a power of attorney authorizing him to get a second permit to take the car out of the country. Nothing persuaded the Panamanian officials, however, who convinced Roger that he wasn't even allowed under local law to drive the vehicle unless I was in the front seat. They hinted darkly that he was in violation of so many laws that the fines would amount to $1500 or more and they could even impound the car.

My intrepid husband didn't panic. He turned right around and drove back to the hotel in David where people very kindly came up with the brother-in-law of the cousin of somebody who agreed to keep our car in his carport, its license plate well hidden behind a potted plant, until Roger's return. My husband trustingly left him all the paperwork on the vehicle and climbed on a bus for Costa Rica.

All the time I was fretting and fussing about not hearing from him in those first few weeks at sea, he was busy swearing everybody at home to secrecy lest I find out about the car and *really* start worrying.

The Monday before the Friday that I disembarked, he was back on the bus traveling through the Isthmus with no idea if he would find the car where he left it. But there it was. Nobody had sold it to a chop shop. He drove it to the airport outside David, parked it in the shade and rented a car to drive to Colón, not wanting to risk being stopped by the police and losing our car forever. While at the airport, he hunted down a Customs official and was referred to a decrepit building a few kilometers down the road. He waited in the appropriate office until he and the official were alone, pulled all the dollars out of his pocket and stuck them in his passport and handed it over. The money fell out on the official's desk behind the counter. The man took pity on him and produced a false entry document that would have allowed the car to remain legally in the country for the almost 60 days it had been parked there, which was just enough time for Roger to pick me up and then take the car back across the border with me in it.

It was wonderful to see him outside the port security gate when I finally got ashore, but after the kiss and hug hello, I asked, "Where's the car?" I will be forever grateful to my husband and to all our friends that I knew nothing of this little adventure while I was at sea. I listened wide-eyed as the whole tale unraveled over a late dinner at our hotel, my admiration for my husband's cool growing by the minute. Two days later we found the car right where Roger had parked it, no parts missing, and our only remaining worry was just getting out of Panama.

It turned out that early Sunday morning was a good time to cross the border. And who should we find to help us through the maze but the same guy who had served as our guide two months before. It was a breeze. We were done in half an hour, during which we both suffered agonies over that false entry document. This time our guide wanted a lot more money for his services than before – he had to give some to his "friend" in one of the offices we had passed through. But we paid it gladly, never so happy in our lives to be finally back on Costa Rican soil. About 100 meters clear of the border I rolled down the window and shouted *"¡Pura vida Costa Rica!"* to the sky and the world at large. I was home.

It turns out that the quality of a destination has everything to do with what you bring to it.

Made in the USA
San Bernardino, CA
08 August 2015